Supporting parents

Supporting parents

Improving outcomes for children, families and communities

Sue Miller

Open University Press

Open University Press
McGraw-Hill Education
McGraw-Hill House
Shoppenhangers Road
Maidenhead
Berkshire
England
SL6 2QL

email: enquiries@openup.co.uk
world wide web: www.openup.co.uk

and Two Penn Plaza, New York, NY 10121-2289, USA

First published 2010

A catalogue record of this book is available from the British Library

ISBN-13: 978-0-33-524176-7 (pb)
ISBN-10: 033524176X (pb)

Library of Congress Cataloging-in-Publication Data
CIP data applied for

Typeset by RefineCatch Limited, Bungay, Suffolk
Printed in the UK by Bell and Bain Ltd, Glasgow

The *McGraw·Hill* Companies

Rahim Khan laughed. 'Children aren't colouring books. You don't get to fill them with your favourite colours'

Khaled Hosseini, *The Kite Runner*

For Keith, Stephen and Kate

Contents

Preface

This is a book that, from my perspective, had to be written. The quality of the relationship between a parent and child has a profound impact on outcomes for children. Understanding our own experiences of being parented is a key to our capacity to parent others. Some of us spend our whole lives trying to make sense of this.

Although I didn't realize when I started, writing this book has been a kind of personal therapy. I think of keeping a journal as a way of making sense of life by getting one's thoughts and feelings down on paper. Having this space to explore what I understand by the development of policy and practice in relation to parenting has been a chance to scrutinize my own knowledge and beliefs. It has allowed me to untangle some, but certainly not all, of the knottier questions in my own experience of being parented and those I continue to ask when I am parenting myself. In many ways, the discipline of organizing this jumbled range of thoughts into a coherent story that has to make sense to an audience I may never meet has allowed me to investigate, define and close a chapter in my own life and provided an impetus to move on to the next.

This means that what you have before you is an intensely personal perspective, the view of the world of parenting that I see when I look at it through my particular lens and my understanding of the research that has been done into the role. As a reader, you won't always see eye to eye with me. I hope you will find yourself bringing your own knowledge and experience of parenting to the text and making your own sense of it.

I've tried to support that process by interspersing and ending each chapter with a series of questions to provide a focus for those debates which you might want to have with yourself, with your loved ones, with your work colleagues, or with your community.

Even though researchers have produced thousands and thousands of words about parenting, being parented is still an intensely personal experience. I would expect that bringing your first-hand understandings of parenting to the text will not only challenge but also enable and empower you to support better outcomes for children and young people in whatever role you undertake.

Acknowledgements

With special thanks to all those I have had the privilege to know and work with over the years who have chosen to be involved in supporting families and parents, including my own, often when we were experiencing some of the toughest of times. Many of you have become close personal friends. You are from a wide range of backgrounds and disciplines but have demonstrated a shared commitment and determination to make things better for all of our children, often in the face of huge challenges and uncertainty. I would urge you not to underestimate the difference that you are making, or the significance of our efforts to work, learn and change the world together.

How to use this book

Although each chapter can be read separately, you will probably get more from this text as a whole if you read them sequentially. Please note that throughout the book, the terms 'parent' and 'parenting' are used to refer to the roles of mothers, fathers and any other primary caregivers.

Key messages about parents' roles and responsibilities in developing positive outcomes for children are covered. Parenting issues are presented as multilayered and complex and relating to matters both within and outside the control of individuals, organizations and national governments. The importance of providing spaces in the home, the community and services for conversations about parenting is explored.

Outcomes for children are described in terms of the five identified in the Children Act 2004 and the UK government's Every Child Matters (ECM) agenda. These state that children should:

- Be healthy
- Stay safe
- Enjoy and achieve
- Make a positive contribution
- Achieve economic well-being.

This book explores the place of parents and parenting education in supporting the achievement of those outcomes and the role of more effective and integrated service provision in leaving a legacy for all family members.

Chapter 1: Does parenting matter?

This chapter reviews a variety of definitions of what constitutes 'good enough' parenting and the ways in which these definitions can be influenced by cultural values. It describes the impact of parenting on each of the five Every Child Matters outcomes and the role that parenting can have in developing intelligence, a sense of self, ideas of right and wrong, confidence and self esteem. The chapter considers the potential impact emotionally, socially and economically of ineffective or inadequate parenting in relation both to individuals and to society as a whole. It discusses the responsibilities of governments and societies for creating the conditions in which positive relationships between parents and children and effective parenting can flourish.

Chapter 2: Parenting: the policy context

This chapter provides an overview of the direction of national policy in the UK throughout the second half of the twentieth and early part of the twenty-first centuries in relation to outcomes for children and safeguarding. In particular, it focuses on the increasing emphasis on the child throughout this period as being a member of a number of different communities: family, school, peer group, locality and the implications this had for the development of integrated conversations about the various perceptions about children's needs and how agencies could work together to meet them. The chapter explores the sense of 'agency' – a growing involvement of different government departments in developing social policy and legislation together that had a direct bearing on family life – alongside the impact this began to have on the perceptions of government's responsibilities in relation to parenting.

Chapter 3: Parenting styles

This chapter focuses on the predispositions and traits of parents themselves and reviews some of the key research findings in relation to individual parenting styles. While emphasizing that there is no one 'right' way to parent, the chapter considers the importance of parents understanding the relationship between what they do and how their child behaves. This is balanced against the significance of risk and resilience factors in the environment as well as the individual characteristics, traits and innate abilities of each child that shape behaviour from within.

Chapter 4: Parenting support: getting the balance right

This chapter describes the different contexts in which parenting takes place and the degree to which:

- government policies create and support or undermine the social and economic conditions for families within which parenting happens,
- communities and local services challenge, support and enable parenting,
- parents embrace and prioritize their personal responsibilities towards caring for the outcomes for their children.

The chapter discusses the implications of these considerations for the workforce that supports parents in their parenting, their training and development and the ways in which services are integrated, organized and delivered within communities. It describes the characteristics of effective parenting practitioners, those individuals with the abilities to both challenge and support parents in their role.

Chapter 5: Making change happen: including fathers and male carers

This chapter describes a model for enabling change in relation to policy and practice around the inclusion of fathers and male carers not only to happen but also to become embedded in service delivery at strategic, organizational and frontline levels.

Taking the theme of father and male carer inclusion, it outlines ways that we can enable leaders and managers, practitioners and families themselves to plan, act and review their work in such a way that they demonstrate that they believe that fathers are just as important as mothers to outcomes for children and have as much right to challenge and support in order to fulfil their roles.

The chapter explores the significance and application of this approach for any leadership team in agreeing priorities, setting service targets and developing the workforce in relation to any aspect of parenting or wider family support.

Chapter 6: Nurturing parents as people

This chapter explores the significance of recognizing the impact of parents' own needs on their parenting capacity and the degree to which the ability of parents to tune in to a child's needs can be affected by the extent to which they have been enabled to tune in to their own. It describes the importance of nurturing parents as people and the impact this can have on their ability to fulfil their responsibilities towards their children. The chapter considers the role and responsibility of governments and societies to listen and respond sooner rather than later to individuals' needs and to pay attention to situations that are likely to damage confidence and self esteem in children and parents. It outlines the significance of these early intervention measures in heading off possible longer-term problems that become embedded in behaviour and can create cycles of poor outcomes for children.

Chapter 7: Letting go: negotiating and facilitating independence

This chapter considers the relationship between the responsibility to control and the freedom to develop independence in the parent–child relationship. It explores the intensely personal nature of individual decisions, relationships and responsibilities that parents seek to balance and also the place of trust and respect within these relationships. The chapter outlines the challenge of making the decisions about when to let go and when to protect a child in a context where what is viewed as good parenting is so variable and discusses the value of developing the dialogue between parents and children around 'making mistakes' and having 'learning opportunities'. The chapter describes the significance of building the confidence in parents and children to listen to and respect each other's roles, responsibilities and needs.

Chapter 8: Leaving a legacy

This chapter is about the legacy that parenting leaves in every individual. It focuses on the significance of providing the space and opportunity for society as a whole to develop a discourse about what we understand by and what we want from parenting and the role of parenting education in enabling and sustaining positive outcomes for children. The chapter explores the significance of our parenting alongside other experiences – education, health, care, friendships – for our collective understanding of who we are, and describes the growing recognition of the way that material, emotional and spiritual poverty can impact on families as a whole. The chapter outlines the place of parents in enabling children to achieve the five Every Child Matters outcomes and to become emotionally intelligent adults with the ability to become effective parents themselves. The result of a focus on supporting children without a simultaneous focus on the adults in the family who are also parents is examined as part of a *Think Family* approach and the chapter reinforces the view that, in relation to outcomes for children, every parent matters. The chapter ends by outlining some of the sustainable and long-standing differences that well-coordinated, integrated and appropriately resourced parenting education alongside family support could make to outcomes for children and the challenges and tensions that are created for governments in considering the degree to which they can or should step into a debate about family life.

1   Does parenting matter?

Key themes
- The different cultural expectations and customs that surround parenting
- Building an understanding and shared view about what constitutes 'good enough' parenting
- The balance of responsibility between individuals and society for parenting
- The importance of parenting for outcomes for children

We might wish to debate the degree to which the way we are brought up or parented, as opposed to factors such as our personality type, predispositions, inherent strengths and resilience, poverty, siblings, peers, culture or environment, influence how we each develop. But academic research and everyday experience indicate that while all of these other factors are extremely important to outcomes for children, parents and parenting behaviours can have a significant impact on each of us. Parenting does matter.

At the most basic of levels, parenting ensures the degree to which we are healthy and safe by regulating our food, shelter and access to care. Parenting stimulates our wider development, our ability to think, problem solve, have confidence, relate to others, become independent. Parenting contributes to our ability to function as part of social groups and society as a whole.

Which of the following do parents do? In your view, which is the most important responsibility for parents and why?

- Keeping children healthy through providing an appropriate diet and helping them access medical support as needed

- Ensuring children's safety, protecting them from harm and avoiding dangers
- Supporting children's learning, getting them to school and providing play and stimulation
- Building children's confidence, listening, encouraging and giving positive feedback
- Developing independence, helping children into employment and establishing their own homes
- Teaching right and wrong, giving moral guidance and setting good examples.

It may not have been from someone genetically related to us but we have all experienced parenting behaviours that have collectively contributed to our upbringing. Even if you are not a parent, you have been parented. You have experienced the impact of parenting on others because this has influenced their behaviour towards you. This in turn is having an effect on how we together shape the environments and the societies in which we all live. If parenting matters, even to some degree, in our individual development, it must also matter to society as a whole.

The impact of parenting on how we develop

The parenting we have each received has contributed to our earliest sense of who we are, how our most basic needs will be addressed, where we will develop our first understandings of human behaviour, expectations of others, roles and responsibilities, sense of right and wrong. Parenting has stimulated our development and helped to shape our view of ourselves and our world.

Think of a memory of something that one of your parents said or did with you as a child. Do you think that action shaped your view of yourself and your subsequent behaviour? What helped to make that happen? Do you think someone with a different personality from your own experiencing what was said or done would have reacted differently?

Although we may see broad patterns of similar parenting behaviours, there are many different parenting situations that children experience. In research terms, the potential data sets to consider in relation to parenting are therefore considerable. They vary according to culture, gender, age, economic circumstances, physicality, cognitive ability, medical knowledge, fashion, time and place.

This diversity and richness of attitudes and beliefs about what constitutes appropriate parenting helps to make the role so potentially demanding and stimulating. It also makes it difficult to clarify what we collectively believe to be 'good enough' in relation to parenting behaviour and how as a society we feel any responsibilities for addressing issues that we might feel influence parenting capacity and thereby support parents to be the best they can be.

In summary, there are a number of challenges to addressing the degree to which individuals or societies can support parents in their role. While we all come into the world with different predispositions and characteristics, parenting contributes to the life experiences that are important to shaping these. So, while there is widespread agreement that many factors influence children's development, nevertheless it feels reasonable to say that a consensus exists that parenting, at some level, matters.

Cultural differences in parenting

We know from research that genetically identical twins separated at birth but parented completely differently have been shown to develop some similar characteristics that appear to transcend their upbringing (Haimowitz 2009). But we also know that their upbringing and the way they are parented plays a significant role in influencing them. Like many social behaviours it is difficult to isolate which factors and parenting behaviours (what parents 'do') have the most influence on how children 'turn out'. In addition to this, separating out parenting from all the other influences on children's development is notoriously difficult. It also may be ultimately unhelpful even to try. There will always be a dynamic interface between all of these factors, with the personalities and characteristics of every individual child and parent ensuring that no two children, even within the same family, have exactly the same outcomes from the parenting behaviours they experience. Parenting takes place in a social, cultural, political, economic and biological context and has to take account of and respond to that.

Can you think of anything that your parent(s) did that has influenced how you behave today or what is important to you? Do you think it matters how you were parented, or would your genetic make-up mean that you would be the same person even if you had been brought up by different parents? Why do you think parents so often comment that they are surprised that although they brought up their children 'exactly the same' they have turned out 'so differently'? Which do you think has more influence: parenting, peer group or the child's personality?

Does how we were parented matter to our view of effective parenting?

Put a topic with a parenting dimension under the microscope – discipline, developing independence, building confidence and self esteem, enabling decision making – and no matter what the books say, we each bring our own experiences and beliefs to bear in trying to understand and interpret the impact of parenting behaviour.

You might, for example, choose to explain antisocial behaviour in children as the result of parents not smacking their children to reinforce right and wrong because that's what your parents did to you and you are not engaging in antisocial behaviour. But we know that while many children engaging in such behaviour have not had consistent, regular discipline, many have been beaten a lot and that does not appear to have succeeded in making them law-abiding citizens. In addition, knowing what seems to work and why in parenting in a given situation is one thing, being able to put it into practice consistently and appropriately and then being able to generalize that learning to other children is quite another.

I talked with a mother recently who had brought up seven children. She said:

> Even though I had seven children, I didn't have a clue how to parent. I thought I was doing all the right things, letting them have what they wanted, giving in to them all the time. It was only when I realized that their behaviour was so bad that I was going to lose them to social services that I started to think about how I needed to change. I needed to

do something different from what I'd been doing in the past and I needed to do something different from those around me, the rest of my family and how I was brought up. But until I got to that point where I was desperate and someone came to help me to think about what I was doing, show me different ways of behaving towards my children and taking responsibility for them, I was just doing what had come naturally, what I'd grown up with myself.

In this situation the mother was facing what, to her, was a crisis. Failing to change her own or her children's behaviour was going to result in her children coming into care. This was something that was unacceptable to her and she was prepared, at this point, to engage in behaviours that she might have tried in the past but had not been able, for a whole variety of reasons, to sustain. It is interesting to note that she needed a clear motivation – in this case the threat of the loss of her children – for her to engage consistently and persistently in behaviours that enabled change to happen. We shall be exploring in later chapters the factors that seem to act as drivers for such changes in parenting behaviours and how these changes can be supported over a long period of time.

What situations have you encountered where a parent or parents have achieved a sustained change in their behaviour towards their children? What acted as the catalyst for change? Did the situation have to become particularly serious before this was possible? Did some significant additional support or change in family circumstances take place to make this change begin to happen? What was or would have been needed to maintain it?

Is parenting behaviour instinctive or learnt?

The issue of whether some aspects of parenting behaviour are instinctive typically relates to the most basic elements of parental responsibility for protecting a child from danger. In the animal kingdom this generally evidences itself in keeping the young from being taken by predators and the parent animal taking risks themselves to provide food or shelter for their offspring.

We expect human parents to protect their children and respond readily to their basic needs as well. We think of it as an indication of mental illness, perhaps postnatal depression or significant psychological disturbance, if a parent becomes unresponsive or unfeeling towards their child's need for food, warmth or shelter to survive. There would be a sense in which we view that disturbance as having overridden what we might describe as the parental instinct to protect the child from harm.

Comparisons between different cultural expectations of parenting however indicate that it is quite difficult to differentiate which parenting behaviours are truly inherent and instinctive and which are learnt (Dwivedi 1997).

Can you think of any changes in expectations around the parenting role that have taken place between your lifetime and that of the previous generation? You might want to think specifically about changes in the expectations around the roles of mothers and fathers for example. Do any of these changes raise questions around what could be described as 'instinctive' parenting behaviours?

There may be some parenting behaviours that are instinctive, but we do absorb ideas about parenting from our earliest years from those who parent us. It may therefore be problematic to rely on effective parenting behaviour developing 'instinctively'.

Without challenge and support to reflect on those parenting behaviours that we have experienced as children from our own parents, we will probably repeat them, whether they are effective or not. Have you ever heard a parent say, 'I sound just like my mother/ father'? Our earliest experiences of parenting enter our consciousness and, unless they are significantly challenged or we experience a very different set of parenting behaviours, they can become our ways of acting towards our own children. I call this learning our parenting 'scripts' and it is probably one of the reasons why we so often do or say things we heard said to us as children.

Is there anything about the way you were parented that you would repeat as a parent yourself? Anything you would do differently? Would you adapt your behaviours in the light of the needs of the individual child you were parenting? Have your views changed about this as a result of any particular experiences, for example encountering different cultural approaches to parenting or becoming a parent yourself?

I am arguing here that our perceptions of what effective parenting looks like, our conceptualization of the parenting role – what it is to be a father or a mother – is embedded in our consciousness through our upbringing and cultural experiences. Experiencing different parenting behaviours can provide opportunities that could enable us to reflect on, understand and be challenged about how those behaviours might or might not have contributed to some of the strengths and difficulties our own children are experiencing in making sense of who they are and how they choose to behave. Such reflections might also influence our understandings of our own behaviours and are often part of the work that parents describe as both challenging and beneficial when they talk to other parents and share their experiences of bringing up their children.

The impact of different family circumstances on parenting roles

We are not necessarily replicating the same situations or expectations about parenting roles and responsibilities in this generation as we had in the last. Family life changed markedly in the latter part of the twentieth century and looks set to continue to do so. This diversity makes the availability of consistent, targeted and individualized guidance about how to parent effectively in a given situation even more difficult to locate. The changes in the expected roles of fathers and mothers, the variations in family dynamics, relationships and how these are organized, the degree to which what constitutes effective parenting is open to public debate have all contributed to this lack of a 'blueprint' for parenting.

We have at least two problems: the traditional supports for learning parenting behaviour by following in the footsteps of the previous generation have been challenged at the same time as our understanding of the impact of parenting behaviour on the underlying psychological development of children has increased. We are living at a point when family circumstances and variations on parenting situations are far more diverse than in the past so there are many different types of families trying to juggle understandings of how to parent in situations very different from the ones that they grew up in themselves.

Parenting and common sense

Let's be very clear from the outset. Confident and competent parenting that produces confident and competent children is *not* 'just common sense'. To suggest that it is denigrates not only the role itself but also every single drop of human energy and emotion that has gone into parenting since the dawn of time. It does a huge disservice to all those mothers, fathers, carers, children and adults who have worked, worried and wept over their parenting experiences. Although it might be argued that it 'keeps things in perspective' by not overcomplicating the role, regarding effective parenting as 'just common sense' produces an environment where it's not OK to say 'I know this is an important job, I want to do it well, but it's tough and I don't know what to do or how to get help to do it.'

How easy do you think it is for parents to ask for help with their parenting? Where might they typically turn to for help and how appropriate, targeted and differentiated to the needs of a specific parenting situation is that support likely to be? Is it your sense that parents are enabled to head off bigger potential problems proactively or do you feel that the balance of support for parents comes too late?

What is very evident in the work with parents that I have experienced is that, in many cases where parents are facing seriously problematic behaviours and relationships with their children, they have been worrying about their child's behaviour for some time. They have generally tried various approaches to dealing with this, many of which reflect either what they experienced as children themselves from those who parented them, or what their friends and family model around them. Most of this learnt behaviour will reflect trial and error and be useful and reassuring, but not necessarily effective.

Many people working with parents who do not know what to do for the best will describe how they find it extremely helpful when they discover that this sense of uncertainty is widely shared and that they are not alone in needing help. They appear to need, and often to value highly, space to think, talk and listen to themselves, their children, other parents. What seems to be key is that they receive accessible and timely help that is non-judgemental, well informed and consistent (Ghate and Hazel 2002).

All too frequently this type of help is reported as not available consistently, persistently or soon enough to parents and problems escalate until such time as, like the mother I spoke to, the family reaches a crisis point. We will return many times to this question: if we accept that parenting is important, why do we not embed space, time and targeted effective support to think about parenting earlier and more consistently into our communities? Why is this most challenging of roles so often described as being experienced as something that is undertaken either in isolation or under the scrutiny of a number of authorities to whom parents tell and retell their stories but who are not perceived as providing constant, targeted, timely or effective challenge and support?

> How do you feel about the idea that parenting is not 'just common sense'? Are there any parenting behaviours that you think should or do come naturally? Is there a place for teaching and adapting parenting skills or should we rely on our parenting 'instincts'? If you feel that there is a place for reflecting on parenting behaviours, where should that learning take place: in families, communities or through parenting interventions? Should it just happen naturally or is someone responsible for making sure it happens and, if so, who?

How do we support parenting?

If parenting does matter for children and society as a whole, how should we be supporting it? Evidence from the field of adult learning suggests that if we want to help ourselves to get better at a job, we need to create an environment where not only is it safe to admit that we need help but also the help is available, accessible and fit for purpose. It is worth reflecting on the degree to which parents can access consistent, well-informed, non-judgemental support and challenge in relation to their parenting in our communities. For most parents, that support needs to be available very close to where they live, from someone they trust and respect, at any time of the day or night, using different models of delivery and before the problems they are facing become so enormous that they are in danger of losing their children altogether.

We will be exploring later the degree to which we are or are not as a society currently succeeding in achieving a balance between supporting the difficulties of parenting, challenging inappropriate or inadequate parenting and being honest about the realities and messiness of human behaviour and relationships which, after all, are at the heart of developing 'good enough' rather than 'perfect' parenting.

> Can you think of any parenting behaviours that you have observed or experienced that you feel are building up problems for later life? To what extent do you feel parents are able to access support from family, friends or professionals for the conversations to help to recognize this? What makes such support effective and how could we measure that effectiveness?

Do we give the impression that we believe that parenting matters?

For a human endeavour to which every society and culture attaches such importance in relation to outcomes for children, we are inconsistent in our expectations about parenting and the ways in which we set about challenging assumptions that we all make about parenting behaviour. Buy any newspaper, walk around any shopping centre, watch any daytime TV, observe the behaviour of any group of professionals who work with families and think about what varied messages we are communicating about our expectations for parenting. Listen to any interaction between a parent and their child or revisit one you can remember from your own childhood and decide how big the gap was between the way each of the people involved viewed the role and its responsibilities. We are very confused about parenting.

If someone from a different cultural background said, 'Show me good parenting', what would you choose to show them? Ask the person next to you on the bus what they would show them. Ask the people you work with. What would your partner show them? What would your children show them? What would the police show them, or social services, or schools or doctors? Would you show them something today that is different from what you would have shown them ten years ago?

What do you think good parenting looks like? In your view what do good parents do and not do? What is the outcome of good parenting? Compare your views with someone that has had a different cultural background and experience of parenting from your own. How do you account for any differences between your values and priorities in relation to parenting?

This is interesting when we consider that we are living at a time when there is such attention from governments, agencies and the media in how children are parented. We often hear that *children are the future* but it would be very understandable if that visitor from another culture were to express some confusion and observe some inconsistencies between what we say and what we do in relation to both childhood and parenting.

Questions to consider

- Even though we possess incontrovertible evidence of the significance of diet on outcomes for children, in some places obesity in children under five is extremely high. To what extent is individual parenting behaviour responsible for this and where are there wider, collective responsibilities relating to society as a whole to both support and challenge parenting behaviour in relation to diet? How do we justify the inconsistencies of allowing targeted advertising on foods known to be bad for children on those children and their parents?
- Research supports the understanding of the significance of creative, exploratory play in the earliest years for brain development and the ability to problem solve and think independently. However, despite the best efforts of successive governments and service providers, what would help us better to target and coordinate resources to provide parents or primary caregivers with the time and determination

to give those sustained activities that we know support and challenge them to develop effective exploratory play in their children, particularly those likely to find developing such abilities most difficult?

- Time and time again parents describe themselves as receiving the kind of regular, embedded, positive, directed, focused and coordinated parenting support they need that sees them engaged responsibly, maturely and emotionally intelligently in the care and upbringing of their children, only when they have found themselves in crisis. Is this really the case, or just an excuse? How could barriers to support be addressed?

- Where does the balance lie between society expecting individuals to provide effective, responsible parenting and creating the conditions to support this to take place? If we truly believe that parenting matters, are we putting our resources sufficiently consistently or rigorously into enabling all parents and especially those parenting in difficult circumstances to do so effectively?

- Why do you think we convey such varied messages about how to care for children? Is it just too hard for us to be consistent or are there too many different agendas and value bases for us to support parenting consistently?

2 Parenting
The policy context

Key themes

- The focus in policy terms on integrating children's services as a way of addressing safeguarding issues
- The growing attention paid to outcomes rather than outputs
- The role of parenting and family support in achieving these outcomes
- The increasing recognition of the link between poverty and poor outcomes

The development of the Every Child Matters agenda

In 2003 five outcomes for children were identified as part of the then New Labour government's policy in the UK for improving support for families. These became known as the Every Child Matters (ECM) outcomes. The government's aim is set out as follows:

> For every child, whatever their background or circumstances, to have the support they need to:
>
> - Be healthy
> - Stay safe
> - Enjoy and achieve
> - Make a positive contribution
> - Achieve economic well-being
>
> (Department for Education and Skills (DfES) 2003)

The start of a new millennium provided an opportunity for a focus on the needs of children in the UK. Arguably some of this focus arose from political concerns around the impact of poor outcomes for children on society as a whole and a growing recognition of the importance of targeting earlier intervention at those family and parenting situations where there was a high probability of future (and almost always very costly) interventions being needed if problems were not headed off sooner rather than later.

A number of challenges were the subject of specific initiatives and became the focus of much policy and practice. These included:

- Developing effective safeguarding behaviours to assess whether children should or should not enter the looked after system
- School attendance
- Teenage pregnancy
- Attainment of five General Certificates of Secondary Education (GCSEs) by school leavers
- Childhood obesity
- Mental health of children
- Childhood poverty.

Was parenting significant for the achievement of the five ECM outcomes? In the UK the message that governments had a role to play in enabling parents to deliver effective parenting and thereby to improve outcomes for children began to receive far greater attention towards the end of the twentieth century and in the early part of the twenty-first century. There were some attempts to quantify the impact of ineffective parenting in terms of outcomes for children's learning, criminality, employment and emotional well-being (Department for Children, Schools and Families (DCSF) 2009d). There was also greater attention paid to the importance of services working in a more integrated way to support parents, and through them, children.

Victoria Climbié

In 2003 the Laming Inquiry focused attention on the death of a young African girl who had lived with her great-aunt in London (Laming 2003). She was eight years old and called Victoria Climbié. Her great-aunt and the great-aunt's boyfriend, who had been responsible at the time for her parenting, killed her.

It was not a quick death; it happened only after she had been tortured and neglected for many months. It was not a hidden death; Victoria was well known to all the agencies that any child in a modern, industrialized, wealthy country can expect to access. She went to school (or was supposed to). She had a general practitioner (GP) and health visitor. She had a bulging hospital file that recorded injury after injury, some of which individually and certainly collectively were suspicious. She had a social worker. She did not live in a remote corner of the British Isles where there were no other people who saw her. She lived in London, in an ordinary street with neighbours and shopkeepers, police, pedestrians, children and young people, other parents – a community. Her great-aunt and the boyfriend attended a local church and she went with them.

What do you think a visitor from a different culture would have made of this? Lots of people may have suspected that Victoria's great-aunt and the boyfriend were delivering grossly inadequate parenting, but she still died. How might that visitor respond to being told that Victoria was not the first child this had happened to, nor would she be the last?

In 2008 the death of another child known generally in the press reports at the time as 'Baby P' would rock the nation. How would that event affect our visitor's perception of the degree to which we turned our belief that parenting matters into activities that could effectively support and challenge parents to fulfil their responsibilities effectively? Although much of the attention following these child deaths turned to the role of the professionals involved in the families, in each case it was the primary caregivers who carried out the killing. In relation to Victoria Climbié would they have assigned different levels of parenting responsibility:

- to her great-aunt and the boyfriend
- to those paid to ensure her safety
- to the members of the wider society in which she was growing up.

Would they have felt that we showed as a society that we should take individual responsibility for ensuring that our own children were parented effectively but that society as a whole was also responsible for helping to create the conditions in which individuals could fulfil those responsibilities to the best of their abilities?

Where do you think the responsibility for Victoria Climbié's death lay? What is your justification for your view?

From 2000 and as a direct response to Victoria's death, the government of the time developed the policy direction known as the *Every Child Matters* agenda in the UK. This agenda focused attention on five outcomes for children, which became the guiding principles for the way services for children were expected to be delivered. They emphasized that all children's services professionals shared a collective responsibility for achieving these outcomes (DfES 2003).

One of the effects of this shift towards a more joined-up approach to service delivery was a need to develop a shared set of perspectives around risk and thresholds for intervention. This proved enormously challenging. The language and practice particularly around safeguarding evidenced that different practitioners had a range of responses and assigned different thresholds when they felt a child was 'in need'. There was some suggestion that these reactions owed much to the availability of the resources at their disposal and an individual practitioner's personal and professional experience rather than any widely shared 'tariff' in relation to assessing need and deciding on a response. As a result families with similar presenting issues might receive differing interventions depending on who they brought these to for help.

Policy focus on parenting

In 2007 the UK government, in response to the growing volume of debate about the role of parents in achieving positive outcomes for children, introduced another policy document called *Every Parent Matters* (DfES 2007).

This time they focused very specifically on outlining a range of government initiatives that had targeted parenting behaviours and the significance to society as a whole of parents being effective in these. They emphasized that knowing how to parent confidently and competently was not 'just common sense'. There was a growing unease about the rise in the number of violent crimes involving young people and the degree of disconnectedness and alienation some young people appeared to be experiencing, in spite of the additional material benefits that many then accessed and the start of a greater focus on 'parenting' as something that government could be seen to have a responsibility to do something about.

Whether poor outcomes for children could be ascribed to poor parenting, low educational achievement, lack of opportunity to move out of poverty (this was also the period when 'narrowing the gap' between those that had wealth and those that did not was receiving increasing attention from politicians at both local and national levels) was hard to decide. For whatever reason, policy makers were becoming increasingly focused on the degree to which the quality of parenting mattered in this debate and whether it would be effective to focus additional and compensatory parenting support specifically on those families that were most 'at risk' of poor outcomes (Martin et al. 2007).

In 2007 the government also brought together sections of two departments that had hitherto worked in parallel – the then Department for Education and Skills (DfES), which became the Department for Children, Schools and Families (DCSF), and parts of the Home Office. They created a project: the Respect Agenda (Home Office 2005) required these two departments to work together on developing, among other things, places in local communities where parents could develop parenting skills.

What this did was to align two government departments that had previously looked at parenting through very different lenses. The DCSF had traditionally adopted a more supportive, enabling and educational approach to parenting issues, spearheading during the 1980s and 1990s initiatives like Family Learning (DCSF 2010b), Sure Start Children's Centres (DCSF 2010f), and parental involvement in children's learning through school (DCSF 2010e). This was the relatively supportive and enabling end of the parenting agenda in government terms and engaged, in the main, with the more confident, less chaotic or threatening parents.

What do you feel might have been the result of bringing together such different cultures in terms of government departments? What might have been the impact of the different priorities and targets that each had on how they chose to view parenting issues? How might the engagement of such different perspectives around parenting have needed to be handled? In your experience, what sorts of activities enable people to build a shared understanding and language to talk about an issue like parenting?

The parenting work offered by the Home Office had represented the 'challenge' end of the parenting support spectrum. If the DCSF traditionally offered what might be described as the 'carrot', the Home Office offered the 'stick' – parenting orders to force parents to address their child's antisocial behaviour or non-attendance at school, compulsory orders relating to behaviours such as domestic violence, drug and alcohol abuse, neglect and ultimately custodial sentencing.

Inevitably the cultures of the two departments reflected the clientele with whom they traditionally worked. Even their literature and the language in which it was described were starkly different: the DCSF fronted most of its documents with colourful pictures of (generally young) children, sometimes playing or studying, whereas the Home Office documents were predominantly much starker and sterner and focused on more troubled aspects of (often teenage) behaviour. Inevitably this juxtaposition of two different cultures gave the potential for some interesting and, I believe, arguably better informed approaches to developing policies that to some extent circled around but aimed to establish confident and competent parenting.

> Do you feel that parents benefit from receiving support that gives encouragement and reassurance about their parenting but that also challenges them to pay more attention and to prioritize their children's needs? Do you think that the balance should change as the children get older or are both approaches relevant for parents with children of all ages? Do you have experience or know of any parenting support that has demonstrated this balance and any that has not? How would you describe the impact of each?

The bringing together of these two departments to consider family and parenting support coincided with and may have informed the tone of the Children's Plan, published towards the end of 2007 (DCSF 2007), the establishment in 2007 of the National Academy for Parenting Practitioners (2009), and the decision in 2008 to fund the roll out of evidence-based parenting programmes.

The Children's Plan emphasized the importance of viewing children as part of families and communities and the significance of services coming together to support these systems to bring up children effectively. It sought to focus the attention of all agencies on the interrelating systems in which children grow up at home, at school and in communities and encouraged practitioners to view these holistically.

The National Academy for Parenting Practitioners (NAPP) had a mission and vision to:

> transform the quality and size of the parenting workforce across England so that parents can get the help they need to raise their children well. Our vision is that all parents who need it should be able to access quality support from trained practitioners capable of helping them to raise their children to be happy, healthy, safe, ready to learn and to make a positive contribution and achieve economic well-being.
>
> (NAPP 2009)

Together these initiatives were emphasizing the policy focus on children as part of families and communities and not just pupils. NAPP's focus specifically as described in its vision statement was on developing the parenting practitioner workforce in order to enable parents to fulfil their responsibilities.

However, the language used was often very future orientated with a focus on children's 'potential', the 'resource' that they represented and their worthiness to receive 'investment'. This could be contrasted at times with situations where the choice of language adopted in literature and debate about children was more associated with children's rights: their entitlement to grow up safe, healthy, happy and secure, the responsibility of adults – whether parents or politicians or practitioners – to establish an environment where this was possible and their entitlement to access the sort of targeted and early interventions and help to be able to do this.

To what extent do you feel that children have a right to experience a positive childhood and that adults have a responsibility to ensure they grow up in an environment that gives them the best chance of achieving this and that parents have an entitlement to support to enable this to happen?

What parenting support was available in communities?

At the same time the government introduced in 2006 in every local authority a new role that had never been identified before: parenting commissioner (DCSF 2010a). The parenting commissioners were to be the professional practitioner managers of the government's parenting policy. They had to lead the way in enabling local authorities to develop the sorts of conditions where effective parenting support would flourish and parents would be better able to fulfil their responsibilities to tune in to their children's needs.

The first task the parenting commissioners had was to develop a Parenting Support Strategy and Action Plan in 2008 that set out how parenting support was going to be carried forward in the particular local authority where they worked.

Plans and policies sometimes look impressive on paper but when it comes to implementing them, very quickly run out of steam, either because they are ill thought through, too ambitious, not sufficiently well resourced or take no account of the skills and abilities of those who are charged with taking them forward. Time would tell the degree to which these strategies actually delivered parenting support in ways, when and to whom it was most needed, but the fact that government required them certainly demonstrated that parenting was on their agenda.

Parenting strategies were required to begin with an audit of the existing support that was available in each area to enable parents to carry out their roles. Figure 2.1 shows a typical spread of some of the services being delivered by a whole cross-section of practitioners and agencies that were likely to be available to parents in 2009/10, either through mainstream or grant funding, and which effectively constituted a 'core offer' of family and parenting support in most areas.

Where do you think that most parents would have received support from in terms of universal, targeted and specialist advice at this time? Try to think about services provided by health care professionals, schools, children's social care, adults' services and the voluntary sector. How might family and friends also have been supporting parenting? Which of these services and supports are still available today? How would you account for any changes that have taken place?

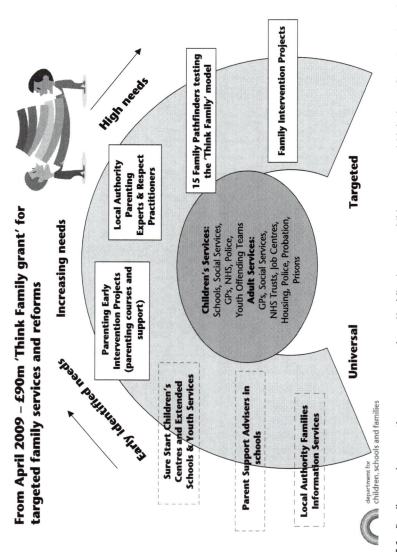

Figure 2.1 Family and parenting support. http://publications.everychildmatters.gov.uk/default.aspx?PageFunction=download options&PageMode=publications&Productid=DCSF-00685-2009&

The strategies varied in quality and the parenting commissioners differed from one another in terms of how they were viewed and positioned within different local authorities. Some parenting commissioners held very senior positions in local authority structures and were able to wield strategic influence over the direction of resources, others were service managers who had resources at their disposal that they could direct towards parenting support activities. Some were little more than coordinators of parenting programmes with very little influence on how services were delivered or where funding was aligned.

> What is your view of the government of the time's decision to develop strategies and action plans in relation to parenting support? Can you see any benefits and any risks? Were parenting commissioners well placed to monitor the differences these interventions were making?

Parenting commissioners did, however, all have access from 2008 to a ring-fenced Think Family Grant that gave each local authority funding directed specifically at parenting support. This funding paid, for the first time, for each local authority to be able to appoint two parenting 'experts' whose roles were to support the parenting commissioners to oversee the quality of the parenting support available in a local authority, to establish staff development and a training pathway for any practitioners providing support to parents, evidence-based parenting programmes that would allow systematic opportunities for parents to develop their parenting skills and Family Intervention Projects (FIPs) that focused on some of the most vulnerable families in communities. Evidence-based parenting programmes include the following:

- Families and Schools Together (FAST)
- Family Links
- Incredible Years
- Mellow Parenting
- New Forest Parenting Programme
- Parenting Positively
- Solihull Approach Parenting Group
- Strengthening Families 10–14 (UK)
- Strengthening Families, Strengthening Communities
- Triple P.

These were targeted towards those parents who were known to have children most at risk of poor outcomes and featured in NAPP's Commissioning Toolkit (NAPP 2010). Part of the Think Family Grant paid for a Parent Early Intervention Pathfinder (PEIP) specifically directed at delivering such programmes, targeted at parents with children aged between 8 and 13 years of age, which had been shown to have a positive impact on outcomes for children.

> Can you research the types of evidence-based parenting programmes that have been supported in the services and communities that you have encountered? What impact have they been felt to have and are they still available now? Who delivers them and how are they accessed? Do they run alongside wider family support and, if so, how is that work coordinated?

Some local authorities gradually moved towards establishing a core offer of fully funded parenting programmes delivered as part of day jobs by a range of practitioners and covering different parenting situations so that there was an appropriate programme available to meet the needs identified by parents.

Figure 2.2 shows an example of one such core offer at the time which aimed to provide parenting programmes funded from a range of sources in an attempt to create a situation where parents could be assured that there was a programme suited to their needs available in the area.

What is the relationship between Every Child Matters and parenting?

Victoria Climbié's death acted as a focus for a UK-wide review of the way in which services for children were organized, how information was shared between them and the degree to which they were clear about what they were trying to achieve. The role of parents in relation to the five outcomes was recognized as significant but there was not a robust means for isolating their influence and measuring that significance. The behaviour of parents and a focus on the skills, time and energy needed to parent effectively was, however, becoming a greater focus of attention in policy terms.

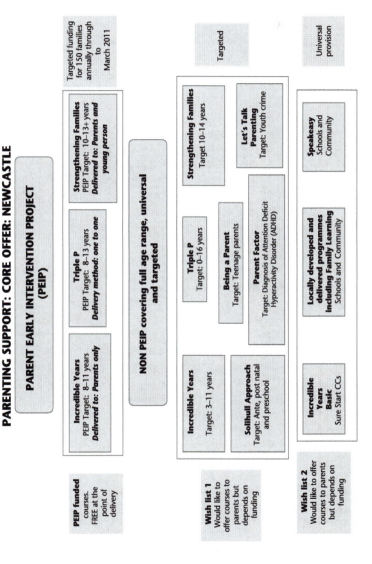

PARENTING SUPPORT: CORE OFFER: NEWCASTLE

PARENT EARLY INTERVENTION PROJECT (PEIP)

Targeted funding for 150 families annually through to March 2011

PEIP funded courses. FREE at the point of delivery

Incredible Years PEIP Target: 8–11 years *Delivered to: Parents only*	**Triple P** PEIP Target: 8–13 years *Delivery method: one to one*	**Strengthening Families** PEIP Target: 10–13+ years *Delivered to: Parents and young person*	

NON PEIP covering full age range, universal and targeted

Targeted

Wish list 1 Would like to offer courses to parents but depends on funding

Incredible Years Target: 3–11 years	**Solihull Approach** Target: Ante, post natal and preschool	**Triple P** Target: 0–16 years	**Being a Parent** Target: Teenage parents	**Parent Factor** Target: Diagnosis of Attention Deficit Hyperactivity Disorder (ADHD)	**Strengthening Families** Target 10–14 years	**Let's Talk Parenting** Target: Youth crime

Universal provision

Wish list 2 Would like to offer courses to parents but depends on funding

Incredible Years Basic Sure Start CCs	**Locally developed and delivered programmes Including Family Learning** Schools and Community	**Speakeasy** Schools and Community

Figure 2.2　Core offer of parenting support.

A great deal of the professional debate over many years had been about services and organizations getting better at sharing what they were doing and why with each other. This had increasingly taken place alongside discussions about how these services could work in a more integrated way with one another and better support and challenge parents to fulfil their responsibilities as well. Significant attention and energy during this period was directed towards addressing the role of integrating services and practitioners in relation to the ECM outcomes. Attention alongside this was also being directed to considering how parents could better step up to their responsibilities in those roles.

Do you think there was more of a focus on regulating the behaviour of practitioners than parents throughout this period? What issues do you think governments might have faced if they had sought to comment on parenting behaviours where there was not a clear child protection issue? How does this impact on the ability to gain attention for early intervention as opposed to heavier end safeguarding?

Joining up services for parents

Parenting effectively is not just about the interactions between parents and their children. Parenting is influenced by the context in which it takes place. It is about the relationship between creating the conditions for those interactions and wider social policy. Parenting is challenging for anyone, but it is especially hard to parent effectively if you live in inadequate housing, take drugs, have mental health problems, poor diet, have inappropriate and/or inconsistent levels of support or were poorly parented yourself. In the UK in the early part of the twenty-first century, thinking about the needs of families as a whole rather than those of the children separately from those of the parents challenged service providers to engage in dialogue about how different policy initiatives interrelated and either made it easier or added to the parenting challenge. This contributed in 2008 to the development of what became known as the 'Think Family' approach with 15 local authorities being identified to act as pathfinders across the country to explore some of the implications of this (DCFS 2010c).

What were some of the issues with which those involved in taking forward this debate were grappling in the early part of the twenty-first century? As a society, we might have wanted parents to go to work, but to do so safely they needed effective childcare. We might have wanted parents to stop living on benefit, but to continue to build effective relationships with their children. To do so they would need flexible working conditions and good quality advice and support about how to build those parent–child relationships. We might have wanted children to develop healthy lifestyles but to do so we would need to develop public spaces where they could play energetically and local shops that supplied cheap, nutritious food and put an end to targeted advertising of unhealthy foods. We might have wanted to see parents developing the knowledge and skills to parent effectively but we needed them to be able to access advice and guidance that was aimed at parents that were isolated or trying to parent in the very circumstances that we knew from research were likely to lead to poor outcomes for their children. We might have wanted to spend resources on children because their development was recognized as crucial to the future of society as a whole, but there might be other demands on our resources, or a reduction in what was available which would mean that they might become less of a priority.

How important is it to join up our social, economic and community development agenda with support for parenting? To what extent do you feel we are sometimes guilty of developing policies that undermine each other, rather than thinking about families as whole units, for example encouraging parents into work outside of the home while wanting them to spend quality time with their children? How should we choose to deal with these tensions?

There was still a question however about how great a share of our collective attention and resources this area of social policy would continue to receive if government could not demonstrate sufficiently robustly that positive change had taken place in the short term, even though there was a recognition that this was an agenda that required everyone to take a longer-term perspective. Sure Start Children's Centres were established through public funding with specific and ambitious objectives to address outcomes for children that were often the product of long-standing and intergenerational conditions that were unlikely to be changed in the sort of timeframes normally allowed to governments.

Our visitor from outer space might hypothesize that where a society focuses its resources and the degree of its commitment to continuing to do so, may say something about what that society values and where it perceives its own responsibilities to lie. The extent to which parenting was viewed as a social and political priority then and the degree to which parents were supported and challenged to fulfil their roles and responsibilities could indicate the significance we attached to the role.

Where are we likely to be directing our resources for parenting support in the future? How significant is the attention paid to parenting and developing close family relationships in our society?

What tensions are there between the various roles and responsibilities that we all choose to carry on outside the home and those we have inside?

What are the conditions that we want to create collectively to enable all parents to fulfil their responsibilities as parents to the very best of their ability?

Did focusing on ECM outcomes and Think Family work?

During the early part of the twenty-first century there was significant reorganization and restructuring both at central government levels and within local authorities in the UK to try to be more integrated and joined up in thinking across children's and adults' services about the support given to children and families. There was emerging evidence from the Family Intervention Projects that where these interventions from adults', children's and parenting services had been robust, persistent and targeted and where staff had been well supported, information shared early and services and families engaged then outcomes were improved (DCSF 2007). There was a very great deal of which to be proud, but the ongoing challenge of keeping attention on early intervention for families and parents at what was a time of enormous changes was such that it was no time to be complacent.

In 2007 the Children's Society, one of the largest voluntary sector organizations in the UK, commissioned a report that identified the

UK as the worst country in the industrialized world to be a child (Layard and Dunn 2009). Think about that for a moment. The UK achieved that rating because of the levels of mental ill health in British children: the rates of stress, depression, bullying, self harm, suicides. The UK also scored high because of the levels of obesity in children. When it was a basic human right to have access to a diet that would be life enhancing, in the UK some families were feeding their children in ways that were actually reducing their life expectancy. The UK also achieved the score for the way that young people were perceived to think about and use their bodies for sex. The UK had achieved a lot, but people could be under no illusions that there were (hardly surprisingly given the complexity of the agenda) still issues to address.

How do you feel about this research? How robust was the data on which it was based? Were the findings conclusive? Does it surprise you that a rich, industrialized country like the UK was apparently producing such unhappy children? Why do you think that was appearing to happen?

If there was ever a moment for parents and parenting support to come centre stage and receive focused and intelligent attention, it had arrived.

Family and parenting support

The early part of the twenty-first century also saw the introduction of a number of policies in the UK that were described as 'family friendly' by a government which was then overseeing an economy that was relatively buoyant. There was investment in childcare facilities, tax allowances to enable families that worked to offset some of their family costs against the costs of using this childcare and some attention being paid to the relevance of employers allowing their staff to adopt flexible working arrangements to accommodate to their family needs.

There was a growing recognition that family support interventions needed to be delivered alongside the parenting support designed to teach the necessary skills, attitudes and awareness parents seemed to appreciate. Parenting programmes, when professionally organized and delivered, provided the space for conversations to deliver the key activities involved in parenting within the context of changing patterns of family life.

> How does parenting support that effectively 'teaches' parenting skills differ from family support? How does parenting support need to exist alongside and take account of family circumstances and what do you see as the benefits of approaching parenting support in this way?

Making parenting matter

There was, at this time, a growing belief that the ability to know how to carry out the parenting role effectively developed better with good quality parenting support interventions delivered by highly skilled and properly trained parenting practitioners. Parents, particularly those trying to bring up children in some of the most challenging of circumstances, were not surrounded by consistent or constructive role models, very often did not have the head space to reflect on how their role was panning out and when they did finally receive consistent, focused support it was often perceived as too late and within a context of statutory intervention because the child had reached a threshold where they were now deemed to be significantly at risk.

At the same time, the average numbers of hours worked in the UK changed for different groups with just over one-fifth working more than 45 hours a week. We also witnessed an increase in expectations for standards of living. The introduction of the minimum wage, while extremely welcome, meant greater competition to produce goods that could challenge on price those imported from those places in the world where workers were paid far less (often, but not always, and ironically, because they were children). Parents often found themselves with less time or energy to focus on just enjoying being a parent.

Where would we find the resources for parenting support?

Parents get support not only from professionals but also from each other, from friends and family, from their own memories of what their parents did for them. Time and time again the research into parenting support reinforced the significance for parents of having that time and space to reflect constructively, persistently and systematically on those understandings in order to better understand their behaviour, their children's and the relationship between the two. Unfortunately, life in the twenty-first century did not always allow parents and children these opportunities. Parenting had always been a demanding role, but having children had been viewed as part of the natural order, a source of mutual benefit for parents and children when families were the primary source of care and support and often hugely rewarding emotionally and psychologically. With an increasing focus on choice, careers outside the home, an awareness of the complexities in the role and the raising of expectations about how to do it 'well' some people began to choose either to delay or never to have children at all.

Are there risks to focusing on parenting skills? Could it lead to a situation where parents are overly blamed rather than supported? Can it overemphasize parenting 'techniques' rather than parenting warmth and enjoyment and give a sense that there is a 'right' and 'wrong' way to parent?

How do you think people who support parents can balance these potentially conflicting messages about learning to be more effective as a parent within a context that demonstrates that, as with any relationship, parents and children will encounter tensions and challenges in their communications at times and need time and space to build the love and trust that underpins all effective relationships?

Happiness and well-being are generated from a number of factors, but being part of a mutually supportive set of relationships is one of these. The family has always been viewed as being at the heart of these relationships, but the family was and had been changing and evolving very significantly throughout the twentieth century. In spite of this, children and their need for boundaries and security within their families still required attention from parents.

It is always difficult for governments to achieve a feeling of well-being in the electorate that is not linked very strongly to economic well-being. Indeed, if the populace is not generating wealth, it cannot provide for itself those services that society as a whole benefits from:

health and social care, education, culture and leisure, early intervention family and parenting support. However, achieving a balance
between work and life in order to ensure individuals enjoyed a feeling
of well-being arising from both was a focus of some debate at the time
with attention being paid to the impact of that stress on adults and
children.

> To what extent do you feel that early in the twenty-first century work–
> life balance might have been problematic for some individuals? How
> much of this could have been linked to an increase in the cost of living
> and greater expectations for material goods and an emphasis on wants
> rather than needs? What impact might that change in cultural expect-
> ations have had on parenting behaviour and capacity?

Of course, for a society to be able to provide high quality education,
health and social care for its citizens, it must be generating wealth.
But it must also decide the extent to which it will direct this wealth
production back into the lives of its citizens.

This is an intensely political question that takes us to the heart
of debates about the tensions between government responsibility
towards the most vulnerable within a society and the need for individuals to take personal responsibility for themselves and their
families.

> If it is a government's job to provide the external, economic conditions
> that will most allow a population to flourish, how far are governments
> responsible for ensuring that a safety net of services funded by the
> wealth generated exists for the most vulnerable as well? Does providing
> such a safety net create a dependency culture and prevent individuals
> from taking personal responsibility for themselves and their families?
> How far should parenting support and 'family friendly' policies work
> hand in hand?

Links between services

We know that parenting in some situations is especially problematic
and that the children of parents with certain sorts of issues are more

likely to have poor outcomes, low attainment, poor school attendance, greater levels of antisocial behaviour and low self esteem. Although these are not the outcomes that family policies and services are entirely accountable for, it makes considerable sense for adults' and children's services to work more closely together to try to head off such difficulties before they become part of a vicious circle of history repeating itself and to build parenting support that is appropriate, accessible and sustainable into any interventions that they deliver.

As the evidence grew about the impact of parenting on outcomes for children, the attention and resources of government began to turn towards what had previously been viewed as an intensely personal issue for individual families to conduct according to their own perceptions and understandings. There were still strong messages in the literature about the complexity of the relationship and interplay between the needs of individual children and the personalities and capacities of different parents. Parenting strategies and parenting commissioners regularly reinforced the view that there was no one 'right way' to parent and that what was needed was the creation of spaces for conversations about parenting conducted in mutually respectful circumstances that both acknowledged and challenged people to think about the significance of parents. This began to be linked through a Think Family policy to a debate about the responsibility of society to provide the kinds of wider contexts in which families could conduct family life safely and securely.

There were no short cuts to achieving this. People providing the support for these conversations about family life and parenting benefited from doing so in the knowledge that they could draw on training and support themselves in order to achieve the balance that was known to be crucial to establishing the kinds of relationships where parents and their children could learn together, develop respect, empathy and mutual acceptance and affection for each other.

However, history shows us that when governments turn their attention to an issue, very often they legislate around issues where previously individuals had been allowed the freedom to act as they saw fit. It can become difficult to have meaningful conversations about complex cause-and-effect factors when those delivering a service are under pressure to be able to demonstrate results relatively quickly, in order to justify further investment in a particular approach. It is only reasonable for there to be evidence of the impact of funding from the public purse that those individuals creating such wealth can review, but it is notoriously difficult to show the impact of social policies that can take generations to work through.

This is a tension that does not sit comfortably with a democratic society where governments are expected periodically to be re-elected on the evidence of their performance in relation to the major issues of the day, whether national security, environment, the economy, health, education, employment, transport, care of elderly people or the safeguarding of children.

Often parents deal with the here and now and may not recognize the potential problems they could be storing up for themselves by 'giving in' for the short term. Likewise it is only with hindsight that we are sometimes able to trace the impact of either failing to address, or only addressing superficially, a social issue that is storing up potentially very expensive or even catastrophic problems for society in the future.

> Does history teach us that problems have to become very serious before society collectively decides that 'something must be done?' Think about this in relation to dealing with obesity in children, their sexual behaviour, antisocial behaviour. How would you characterize the way we respond as a society at such issues? What factors motivate us as a society to prioritize them? Is what we then do to address them carried through realistically or for long enough and sufficiently tenaciously or does it sometimes appear we are looking for or overselling a quick fix solution that does not pay sufficient attention to how different factors collectively create problems? Does this matter?

Narrowing the gap

We know that poverty, housing and family circumstances all impact on parenting capacity and the ability to meet children's needs. Very often those needs have been developing over a very long time and, if dealt with sooner, would arguably not have escalated to the point where now not only the parent but also the child needs dedicated specialist help.

Parents have some control over these factors. However, education, employment and financial resources are all linked to the amount of choice and control any individual may have over the circumstances in which they live. Opportunities to change these were still, in spite of everything that had been done to improve access to the means to lift individuals out of relative poverty through improved education and training, still presenting challenges at this point in time. Societies were still filled with inconsistencies and differences of opportunity.

Much was written during this time about the importance of narrowing the gap between people's respective life chances. Enabling parents to aspire for more for their children than they have achieved themselves in terms of not only material benefits but also social and emotional benefits while at the same time creating the conditions for those aspirations to grow could be said to be at the heart of social and economic policies of any responsible government, whatever its political persuasion.

What are your feelings about the profile of parenting support and evidence-based parenting programmes in the UK early in the twenty-first century? From your perspective had government got the balance between supporting parents to do the job confidently and leaving them to fulfil their responsibilities competently right or wrong?

Questions to consider

- What would you show a visitor to your community that was good mothering and why would you choose that?
- What would you show a visitor to your community that was good fathering and why would you choose that?
- Do the differences between the two, if there were any, matter?
- Where do you feel the responsibility lies when a child dies through neglect in the UK? Can you explore the reasons for your answer?
- Does it matter that the UK did so badly in the Children's Society's survey? From your perspective, what could be the implications if the trend continued?
- How important is it for policies that focus on developing parenting support to be related closely to the impact of policies aimed to narrow the gaps that exist economically between different parts of a community?

3 Parenting styles

Key themes
- The different styles of parenting
- What the research has to say
- Emotional coaching and building resilience
- The goal of good enough parenting

Having established that parenting does matter and is important for achieving positive outcomes such as those described by the Every Child Matters policy for children, we are going to move on to consider different parenting styles, their relative merits and demerits, and how we can best support those that have been shown in the research to be the most effective in building resilience in children. Although the various cultural approaches we have discussed suggest that there is no one 'right way' to parent, there is plenty of information about behaviours that are not helpful and activities that are helpful in terms of parenting styles.

We have established that different cultures and beliefs affect the things that parents do when bringing up children. Do you also think there are different styles of parenting: are some parents more laid back, are some stricter? Do factors such as gender ('men are stricter than women'), age ('teenagers are too young to parent') or marital status ('single parents are easy going') affect these behaviours or are these just stereotypes?

For some time psychologists have been interested in the different styles of parenting, the approach that parents adopt consciously or unconsciously in relation to their interactions with children and what this does to the child's view of him/herself, their confidence and emotional well-being. These psychologists believe that parents teach their children how to make sense of the world but in doing so they also provide the child with a view of their own place in that world and how they might best be able to live within it.

Some researchers are particularly interested in the relationship between how children's attitudes and beliefs about emotions in turn shape how they respond to the feelings they have themselves and the emotions of others. They explore what happens when children experience upbringings where emotions are dismissed or appear not to be given any importance and the impact that has on their ability to deal with their own emotions and to recognize and respond to the feelings and needs of others.

We shall consider the work of two psychologists who have produced particular insights into this area: John Gottman and Diana Baumrind. John Gottman (1997) refers to these attitudes towards our feelings as 'meta-emotions'. His work explores the following premises:

- If we attend to our emotions, we are more likely to notice the emotions of others.
- If we fear or neglect our own emotions, we are more likely to fear or neglect the emotions of others.

Gottman (1997) describes four basic parenting styles in his research on families and the emotional climate in the home. He believes that the more parents recognize their parenting styles, the better able they are to understand and do something about the quality of the interactions they were having with their children. Gottman's identified parenting styles are:

- The dismissing parent
- The disapproving parent
- The laissez-faire parent
- The emotion-coaching parent.

The dismissing parent

Emotion-dismissing parents often view their own emotions and their child's as voluntary, as something they choose to feel. When a child experiences a negative emotion, the child should 'decide' to have a more positive emotion. Emotion-dismissive adults tend to think of negative emotions as poisonous, as if these feelings should be avoided.

If a child experiences a negative emotion they will seek to move the child out of the negative emotional state.

This approach can appear on the surface to have some merit. Children learn to control their feelings to the extent that they do not show them and this has some appeal. A child who is not showing that they are upset, frightened, ashamed or anxious is not putting any pressure on a parent to respond to those feelings. There could be many reasons why the parent cannot or does not want or feel able to respond to such emotions. They may feel guilty themselves: acknowledge that this child is feeling sad and it may mean acknowledging some responsibility for that sadness; recognize that the child is scared and it could mean that the parent has to take responsibility for having been neglectful in some way.

Dismissing feelings constantly creates an impression in children that their feelings do not matter, however, and this does nothing positive for their self esteem.

Scenario

Ceri is six years old. She drops her ice cream and bursts into tears.

Parent response 1: 'Stop crying Ceri! It's only an ice cream!'
Parent response 2: Hugs and comforts Ceri.

Think about the impact of these two different reactions on:

- Ceri
- her parent
- their relationship.

The disapproving parent

Disapproving parents view emotions as a matter of personal choice. The parenting responsibility is to stop the child from feeling this way. Generally, strong emotions are not fully under our control as this would suggest. Some of our emotional thinking goes on unconsciously, influencing how we feel about people or leading us to make certain choices. Emotions may be redirected but cannot and arguably should not be just 'turned off'. Doing so can lead to children having such experiences of emotions alone, and lead to them feeling wrong or unacceptable for how they feel.

It is very easy to forget that we all need to learn to understand and develop our feelings about behaviours in ways that are age and socially appropriate. Just because we make a transition to a new stage or role we have not necessarily gained all the necessary skills to manage successfully those feelings at that stage.

Children have to deal constantly with feelings associated with such changes in role and status, both real and perceived: 'You're the big brother/sister now', 'You're at high school now', 'You've left school now', 'You might think you're an adult, but you still live under this roof', 'You're a parent yourself now'. With each change it is easy to expect the child not only to know how to feel but also to be able to understand these new feelings when they may not have had any opportunity to develop these understandings beforehand.

We expect to take time to learn to do most things: to ride a bike, to read, to play the piano and recognize that these skills need to be learnt and practised step by step with rewards and encouragement and to be taught by someone with enthusiasm and skills themselves. How strange that we sometimes behave as if the far more complicated issue of understanding our feelings can be learnt effectively from imperfect and confusing role models and overnight.

Scenario

Tony is 16. He has left school and does not have a job. He sleeps in late and does nothing to contribute to the domestic needs of the house. When challenged he appears angry and depressed.

Parent response 1: 'You're an adult now! It's about time you stopped behaving like a child and learnt to take on your responsibilities.'

Parent response 2: 'This is a big change for you and I bet you don't quite know how to deal with this.'

Think of the impact of these two different reactions on:

- Tony
- his parent
- their relationship.

It is often very much easier, from the outside, to see how particular parenting behaviours are storing up possible problems for the future. When parents are disapproving of a child's feelings, they are effectively conveying a message that these feelings are wrong. In fact, although the feelings might not be particularly useful or constructive they are nonetheless real. It is important to introduce an element of fairness into the expectations that we have for children. Like us, they find change, however inevitable, difficult.

The laissez-faire parent

Parents with a laissez-faire attitude accept emotions as natural and normal. Rather than ignoring their child's feelings, or dismissing them, these parents view emotions as a normal part of life that should be allowed to flow.

'Laissez-faire' adults are not 'hands-off' parents. They value being involved in their children's lives, accept, love and respect them and encourage and honour their children's feelings and self expression. They strive to provide unconditional love and fear that setting limits on a child's behaviour might make the child feel that the parents' love is dependent on their compliance or good behaviour rather than on the child's intrinsic worth.

Do you ever get the sense that sometimes it is hard for parents to say 'No' to their children? Where does this tension arise between wanting to show a child that they are valued beyond price and being unable to take responsibility for just saying no? Why do parents struggle sometimes with assuming authority in the parent–child relationship?

Could it be that, unlike in the past, we are far more aware of the frailty of people in authority and less willing to assume that authority ourselves as a result? We live in a society that values freedom of expression and opportunity, choice and diversity. But the consequent increase in laws, restrictions, age limits and enforcement agencies suggests that in general we have found this freedom difficult to handle responsibly. The more honest we are about our shortcomings, the easier it becomes to wonder 'Who am I to tell my child how to act – I can't even manage my own life effectively?'

Scenario

Lena is 14. She is moody, rude and destructive and manages to annoy and upset most of her family at any important occasions by appearing to resent being asked to take any part in these.

Parent response 1: 'It's her age. I was exactly the same at 14. If she doesn't want to take part we shouldn't make her.'

Parent response 2: 'You have needs and we respect that, but we have needs too. As a parent I'm responsible for teaching you about this.'

Think of the impact of these two different reactions on:

- Lena
- her parent
- their relationship.

It is one thing to recognize where these feelings that children may be experiencing are coming from and to view them as natural. However, there is also a need to help children to see how their behaviour impacts on others so that they are in a position to make their own choices about how to behave in possession of the full information about the consequences of what they are doing. When parents do not succeed in doing this, their children may grow up to need external reinforcement for acceptable and unacceptable behaviour because they will not have these inner controls.

The emotion-coaching parent

The emotion-coaching parenting style best nurtures a child's emotional development. It revolves around showing empathy – valuing and sharing the feelings the child experiences. It means viewing emotions, even negative ones, as a natural part of life.

Empathy is at the heart of parenting and caregiving. It creates resilience, a foundation for strong, healthy, trusting relationships between parent and child. Children who experience this style of parenting learn to recognize, trust and manage their own emotions. They tend to do better in school, have healthier friendships, and recover more quickly from strong emotional events. Children who experience empathy from their parents and caregivers thrive.

It is perhaps obvious, but this approach expects the parent to be tuned in to their child, to be present certainly emotionally and probably physically and to be comfortable with the inevitability of the emotional rollercoaster that is part and parcel of relationships and growing up.

We should not underestimate how difficult it is to carry this parenting style through. Parents slip into habits, react in the moment, get tired, are bombarded with messages about what could happen to their children if they are too firm or not firm enough. Emotional coaching is more about listening than talking and focuses on enabling rather than controlling.

Scenario

Terry does not want to go to school because he says it's boring.

Parent response 1: 'You don't need to tell me! I hated school – it's a complete waste of time. You don't need to bother with school today.'

Parent response 2: 'I can see you're not enjoying school at the moment. Do you think it has any good parts as well as the bad? Do you think going to school might help you in the long run?'

Think of the impact of these two different reactions on:

- Terry
- his parent
- their relationship.

To summarize, it could be argued that parents walk a very challenging line between loving their children and yet at the same time showing that they have a responsibility for shaping their children's behaviour and enabling them to develop the abilities to make their own choices in a personally and socially responsible way.

Do you recognize any of the features of these parenting styles in behaviour you have encountered in parents you know? What impact do you think each parenting style might have on outcomes for children? How significant is the personality of the individual child in either offsetting or exacerbating those impacts?

Diana Baumrind also outlines four parenting styles in her research (Baumrind 1967):

- Neglectful parenting
- Permissive parenting

- Authoritarian parenting
- Authoritative parenting.

Neglectful parenting

At its heart, neglectful parenting does not pay attention to a child's needs. Truly neglectful parenting that reaches thresholds where children are at risk of significant harm is covered within UK legislative frameworks and as a society we expect children to be protected from such behaviours. Indeed, society as a whole can become exercised when children are not protected from significant harm, particularly where risks are known about or being monitored by professionals. We view the needs of children as paramount in such circumstances, although we know that, by and large, it is better for their outcomes if we can reinforce and develop the parenting skills within their own families rather than taking them into the care of the local authority.

Should neglectful parents be punished or supported to develop the skills they need to care for their own children rather than having them taken away from them? What features would you expect to see in such a programme of support, should it be available? How far should any society be prepared to tolerate ineffective and dangerous parenting before intervening?

Permissive parenting

The **permissive** parent attempts to behave in a non punitive, accepting and affirmative manner towards the child's impulses, desires, and actions. She [the parent] consults with him [the child] about policy decisions and gives explanations for family rules. She makes few demands for household responsibility and orderly behaviour. She presents herself to the child as a resource for him to use as he wishes, not an ideal for him to emulate, nor as an active agent responsible for shaping or altering his ongoing or future behaviour. She allows the child to regulate his own activities as much as possible, avoids the exercise of control, and does not

> encourage him to obey externally defined standards. She attempts to use reason and manipulation, but not overt power to accomplish her ends.
>
> (Baumrind 1966: 889)

It is probably easy to characterize this approach as extremely attentive parenting, but it is not conveying that while the child may have needs, so does the rest of the world. While it is to be expected that the very youngest children either developmentally or by age will be extremely egocentric and demanding, we should expect that as children grow they become increasingly aware that they are members of wider groups and need to learn to coexist and support themselves as well as others.

> How far would this parenting style support the development of mutual respect between parent and child?

Authoritarian parenting

> The **authoritarian** parent attempts to shape, control, and evaluate the behaviour and attitudes of the child in accordance with a set standard of conduct, usually to an absolute standard, theologically motivated and formulated by a higher authority. She [the parent] values obedience as a virtue and favours punitive, forceful measures to curb self-will at points where the child's actions or beliefs conflict with what she thinks is right conduct. She believes in keeping the child in his place, in restricting his autonomy, and in assigning household responsibilities in order to inculcate respect for work. She regards the preservation of order and traditional structure as a highly valued end in itself. She does not encourage verbal give and take, believing that the child should accept her word for what is right.
>
> (Baumrind 1967: 890)

There are many examples of parents who would say that they take their responsibilities in relation to setting boundaries very seriously indeed. They work hard to police their children and may well be told they are a 'credit' to them. The concern, of course, is what happens when these restrictions are either not there any more, for instance when the child is no longer under their parent's watchful eyes, or if the child challenges the basis on which the parent is making these decisions.

> How far does this style develop a child's abilities to make their own decisions? What might be some of the underlying values and beliefs that could encourage a parent to adopt this parenting style?

Authoritative parenting

> The **authoritative** parent attempts to direct the child's activities but in a rational, issue-orientated manner. She [the parent] encourages verbal give and take, shares with the child the reasoning behind her policy, and solicits his objections when he refuses to conform. Both autonomous self-will and disciplined conformity are valued . . . Therefore she exerts firm control at points of parent-child divergence, but does not hem the child in with restrictions. She enforces her own perspective as an adult, but recognizes the child's individual interests and special ways. The authoritative parent affirms the child's present qualities, but also sets standards for future conduct. She uses reason, power, and shaping by regime and reinforcement to achieve her objectives, and does not base her decisions on group consensus or the individual child's desires.
>
> (Baumrind 1966: 891)

This parenting style will very often be reflected in a parent who asks questions rather than tells and where the parents will be able to provide an explanation for the views that they hold and not be afraid to have these views explored and challenged. The approach is characterized by an underlying confidence based on a rounded reflection on situations, context, personal characteristics and a willingness to adapt parenting behaviour in the light of these ever changing circumstances as the child matures.

> To what extent do you feel that authoritative parenting styles contribute to a child's sense of security and ability to empathize with others?

Effective parenting support therefore could involve creating spaces for parents, either individually or with others, to think, talk and reflect on their parenting style, the relationship and interactions that they and their children are having in the here and now and to consider their longer-term impact. While most parents are capable of adopting any of these different parenting styles at different times, the reality of everyday life is often that we all slip into habitual behaviours that come most easily to us, whether because of our personalities and genetic predispositions or because of our upbringing and environment. Recognizing this can be a first step in the change process, but doing something about it in a sustained way is considerably more difficult, and the subject of Chapter 4.

Where do you think these parenting styles, if they exist, have their origins? To what extent are they the product of the way that individuals have been parented themselves and how far are individuals genetically predisposed towards behaving in certain ways? What are the implications for the way that we support parents?

Paying attention to our parenting styles and behaviours influences the style of relationship and dynamic between parents and children. Over time they establish, often without us realizing it, behaviours and 'scripts' that can become difficult to change. How often do we recognize in ourselves or observe parents that miss what's happening 'off camera' while busy focusing on other needs: our work, our love life, our finances, another child or family member? It is very difficult to pay attention to or even do anything about the impact of one element of a situation on a wider context without a significant amount of focused energy.

Failure to connect with these most important of interactions between parents and children until the situation is in crisis can lead to behaviours in parents and children becoming embedded and much harder to change.

Implications of using different parenting styles

Parenting has often been described as one of the most fulfilling but also toughest jobs in the world. The parenting styles that have been outlined and the impact that they can have seem to highlight issues that we need to consider about the quality of the attention that parents are being enabled to give to their role. This will reflect a number of issues:

- Parental awareness and understanding of the impact of these styles on outcomes for their children.
- The capacity of parents to do anything about this, even when they are aware of that impact.
- The quality of support that parents have around them.
- The level of significance that parents and society in general attaches to their role and responsibilities in relation to the outcomes for their children.

What do you think could be the outcome for individual children that experience each of these different parenting styles? How likely are they to be able to be healthy, stay safe, enjoy and achieve, make positive contributions, achieve economic well-being? To what extent will it depend on the personality of the individual child? How important do you think wider environmental factors are in mitigating the impact of these individual parenting styles? Note your answers in the table below.

Parenting style	Authoritative emotion coaching	Authoritarian disapproving	Permissive laissez-faire	Negligent dismissive
Style of attention	Consistent	Surveillance	Minimal	Negligible
Level of attention	In focus	Zoomed in	Roving	Off camera
Potential outcome				

The goal of good enough parenting

We could be described as drawing on these different parenting styles to deliver what has come to be referred to not as perfect but as 'good enough' parenting. Bruno Bettelheim (1987) said many important things on the subject:

- The only effective way to help well-intentioned, intelligent persons to do the best they can in raising their children is to encourage and guide them always to do their own thinking in their attempts at understanding and dealing with their child-rearing situations and problems, and not to rely blindly on the opinions of others.

- The good enough parent, in addition to being convinced that whatever his child does, he does it because at that moment he is convinced this is the best he can do, will also ask himself: 'What in the world would make me act as my child acts at the moment? And, if I felt forced to act this way, what would make me feel better about it?'

- The good enough mother, owing to her deep empathy with her infant, reflects in her face his feelings; this is why he sees himself in her face as if in a mirror and finds himself as he sees himself in her. The not good enough mother fails to reflect the infant's feelings in her face because she is too pre-occupied with her own concerns, such as her worries over whether she is doing right by her child, her anxiety that she might fail him.

- Among the most valuable but least appreciated experiences parenthood can provide are the opportunities it offers for exploring, reliving, and resolving one's own childhood problems in the context of one's relation to one's child.

- To be told that our child is 'normal' offers little solace when our feelings are badly hurt, or when we worry that his actions are harmful at the moment or may be injurious to his future. It does not help me as a parent nor lessen my worries when my child drives carelessly, even dangerously, if I am told that this is 'normal' behaviour for children of his age. I'd prefer him to deviate from the norm and be a cautious driver!

- The goal in raising one's child is to enable him, first, to discover who he wants to be, and then to become a person who can be satisfied with himself and his way of life. Eventually he ought to be able to do in his life whatever seems important, desirable, and worthwhile to him to do; to develop relations with other people that are constructive, satisfying, mutually enriching; and to bear up well under the stresses and hardships he will unavoidably encounter during his life.

- The parent must not give in to his desire to try to create the child he would like to have, but rather help the child to develop – in his own good time – to the fullest, into what he wishes to be and can be, in line with his natural endowment and as a consequence of his own life history.

(Bettelheim 1987)

Good enough parenting could be said to be both a destination and a process. Either way, we would never dream of setting out on a journey without knowing where we wanted to end up. If good enough parenting is an end-point of parenting behaviour or the process by which we parent, effective parenting support should enable parents to achieve it.

While we have established that the parenting styles reflect and lead to different parenting behaviours (they characterize what we see and hear parents actually doing), good enough parenting is a standard of behaviour that will be demonstrated by adopting these behaviours to some extent or other. It is what could be said to have been achieved when the balance between the parenting styles is such that the parenting behaviour as a whole has done what it can to achieve positive outcomes for children.

> If parents adopt the most effective parenting styles, will this guarantee positive outcomes for children? Does that mean that if children's outcomes are poor that parents are to blame or are there other factors to consider?
> Explain your answer.

Risk and resilience

Statistics have long been able to demonstrate that certain factors such as education or poverty lead more or less predictably to positive or negative outcomes for children. Yet we know that there are individuals who have overcome seemingly insurmountable odds relating to their birth and upbringing and achieved amazing outcomes. It is tempting to want to identify the factors that play the most significant part in ensuring that children grow up to be happy and healthy. Indeed, governments of all political shades can view themselves as being responsible for creating the sorts of conditions in which this will happen and will develop a whole host of strategies for doing so.

Parents have similar responsibilities and a degree of control, particularly when children are young, over factors in the environment that have an important part to play in whether children can be healthy, stay safe, enjoy and achieve, make a positive contribution or achieve economic well-being. They can never eradicate every risk, nor make their children entirely resilient to whatever life throws at them. But there is sound evidence that the extent to which children experience parenting styles that guide rather than dictate, coach rather than control and develop in children the ability to make healthy rather than unhealthy choices then the more able children are to deal effectively with and adapt wisely to the unforeseen as well as the predictable challenges in life.

Obstacles in any career are inevitable and the parenting career is no different. We should expect difficulties and challenges to be there from time to time. We should expect sometimes to feel completely lost. We will always need help and support. In Chapter 4 we will be exploring the nature of effective parenting support that does encourage good enough parenting.

Questions to consider

- To what extent do you think that parenting styles have a place in helping children to be confident and emotionally secure and how much do you think is the child's personality and predisposition?
- Are parents responsible for their child's emotional well-being, or is it sufficient for them to ensure that they are safe and healthy? Is there an age or stage in a child's life when the parent is no longer responsible or when the responsibilities reverse? If parents are responsible for their children's emotional well-being, safety and health, how equipped are they to fulfil this duty? If they are not responsible, then who is?
- To what extent do you believe that understanding the impact of different parenting styles can help parents to change? What might help to sustain any changes in parenting behaviour, what might undermine these changes?
- How do you think children could be supported to respond to the parenting styles that they are experiencing? Would bringing children and parents together to explore the impact of the parenting behaviour on how children feel and behave be useful?

4   Parenting support
Getting the balance right

Key themes

- Availability of parenting support
- Balancing support and reassurance with challenge and consequences
- Being solution rather than problem focused
- Developing parenting practitioners
- Delivering evidence-based parenting programmes

Most parents get along perfectly comfortably for most of the time. But all parents have times when they need advice about how to handle some aspect of their relationships with their children and some parents, for a whole host of reasons, need access to more of that kind of advice than others.

Parenting capacity has been shown to be affected by factors in a number of different contexts: society as a whole, the local community, the family and the child or the parent themselves. All of these together create the context in which parents form their relationships with their children and carry out their roles and responsibilities. We will be exploring the ways in which these various factors work together to either sustain or undermine the ability of parents to fulfil these roles and responsibilities.

What are parents expected to do? Here we have an imaginary job advert for the role. Would you apply?

WANTED: a responsible person, male or female, to undertake a life-long project. Candidates should be totally committed, willing to work up to 24 hours daily, including weekends, during the initial 16-year period. Occasional holidays possible, but may be cancelled at no notice. Knowledge of health care, nutrition, psychology, child development, household management and the education system essential. Necessary skills: stress management and conflict resolution, negotiation and problem solving, communication and listening, budgeting and time management, decision making, ability to set boundaries and priorities as well as providing loving support. Necessary qualities: energy, tolerance, patience, good self-esteem, self-confidence and a sense of humour. No training or experience needed. No salary but very rewarding work for the right person.

(Pugh et al. 1994: 40)

Which elements of this job description seem to you to be:

- most surprising?
- most challenging?
- most significant?
- most evidenced in parents you know?

Definitions of parenting support

We need to be clear about what we are talking about when we refer to parenting support. Potentially the term covers a whole range of activity, but for the purposes of this discussion parenting support means: *those activities that help parents to develop the skills to carry out their parenting role.* These opportunities might take place on a one-to-one basis or in a group, in a family home or a community-based facility such as a school, clinic or local centre. Parenting support will often take place alongside, but is not the same as, family support.

Parenting support activities encourage the conditions for positive parent–child relationships to develop. They might include informal conversations, outreach and engagement work to build relationships and trust between the parent and the parenting practitioner with a view to supporting confident and effective parenting behaviours, individual discussions about, modelling of and joint carrying out of activities or group based parenting programmes.

Building relationships

The extent to which there is investment in terms of time, energy and resources in outreach work that builds engagement and trust between the parents and those providing parenting support is fundamental to the impact of any support that is available. No matter how well intentioned the support is it will be more effective if parents are motivated to engage. Sometimes practitioners speak about the difficulties they experience in engaging parents that they feel would really benefit from support. What they generally mean is that, from their perspective, there is some problem related to the parenting behaviour that is building up under the surface that they can see will bring problems in the future if not addressed. This may not be the current priority for the parent, but they think it should be and they are struggling to get that message across.

> To what extent do you feel it is important to negotiate the commitment of parents and their children to any proposed change programme? What strategies might enable this to be achieved?

This is tricky territory. Someone has a view but, in order for that view to result in a change of behaviour, everyone involved has to come to a shared perspective about it and this in turn needs to lead to agreed actions. It is always difficult for such collaborations to be reached in any circumstances, but where parenting is concerned this is even more problematic. Who, after all, are you to judge my parenting behaviour?

> What dangers can you see in a professional, friend or family member trying to offer parenting support to a parent who does not perceive there to be a problem, is afraid that they may be judged and found wanting, or perceives themselves as either unable or inappropriately placed to assert themselves in the parenting role?

Family support is very different from parenting support, although there can be similar issues around judgements and perceptions. Family support covers activities such as advice about a wide range of factors likely to impact on family life, for example finances, housing and homelessness, employment, childcare, mental and physical health, drug and alcohol use, domestic violence and family breakdown. All of these provide the context in which parents are carrying out their roles and will have an impact on parenting capacity so it is essential that any parenting support is delivered alongside family support and that the entire package is tailored and responsive to the individual circumstances of the family as a whole.

How important do you think it is to take account of the impact on parenting capacity that an adult having a drug and alcohol problem or debt issues could be having? To what extent do you feel, in practice, that practitioners working with adults address their needs as parents? How might the extent to which we think about family *as a whole* be impacting on how we deliver services and therefore outcomes for children?

What does effective parenting support look like in society?

Parenting, as the job advert earlier suggests, is a challenge. All parents, from time to time, will feel the need for support – someone to complete or share practical tasks like preparing meals, getting children dressed and undressed as well as helping with more developmental activities involving playing, talking and listening.

While much of this support will involve empathizing and listening to the issues that are being addressed and simply sharing the workload, there will also be elements which shape and steer parenting behaviour, provide different models and solutions, question and challenge. This is in effect 'teaching' parenting skills and behaviour and developing parents that reflect on the impact of their actions – individuals able to mix and match different strategies and techniques to achieve positive outcomes for their children in a range of different circumstances. It might happen through general conversation while actually looking after the children, when having coffee and a chat while the children are elsewhere, or through a more systematic raising of awareness and skills development process tied to some kind of intervention.

Parents receive and absorb 'advice' about their parenting informally all the time, often without realizing it, from the behaviours they observe around them and their own experiences of being parented. We might wish to argue that it is entirely their own decision which of these behaviours they choose to adopt or reject and that families should be left alone to bring up their children entirely as they see fit. However, in a society where individuals are closely dependent on the consequences of each other's actions, it is likely that we will always make judgements about, and that governments will be interested in, the quality of parenting based on the evidence of the outcomes for children's behaviour and the impact this is seen to have on society as a whole.

From where do you think parents receive their support and is this different from the situation that might have existed in their grandparents' time?

Children who are not taught or do not develop an ability to make healthy choices about their diet, for example, can grow up to have health problems that can cost society as a whole dearly. Without developing in children the ability to take personal responsibility for behaviour and to consider the impact of one person's actions on others, we create individuals who could be chaotic or dangerous and may eventually require the force of highly expensive external authorities to maintain law and order.

It is because we are so interrelated that it is increasingly difficult not to be interested and affected by the behaviour of others, particularly the behaviour that we learn from those closest to us. We begin to absorb these behaviours from our earliest years and it is not just governments, schools or the criminal justice system but parents, consciously or unconsciously, who play a role and are generally perceived – particularly when their children are young – to have a responsibility to model and moderate what children experience and how they behave as a result.

Are parents always responsible for their children's behaviour? At what stage do other influences – peer group, media, personality – take a greater role in shaping how they act? When are parents absolved of these responsibilities?

Characteristics of effective parenting support

We have paid significant attention in recent years to the development of a range of practitioners with knowledge and skills relating to supporting children's development. As a result we have a children's workforce bridging health, education and social care that is multi-faceted, highly skilled and able to bring a range of insights and perspectives to the assessment of children's needs.

We have regulated the training and accreditation of this work-force and, by and large, working with children is seen as a graduate level profession with higher education and qualification bodies play-ing a significant role in developing and quality assuring their work.

Contrast this with the place of the training and accreditation of the parenting practitioner workforce. While working with parents will appear as an aspect in the training of many members of the children's workforce, there was not an established training pathway specifically designed for parenting practitioners at the early part of the twenty-first century. A whole range of different modules and courses that practitioners dipped into existed but these were almost always accredited below undergraduate level even though those completing them would, often, be qualified professionally to beyond this point.

The National Academy of Parenting Practitioners was established in 2007 with specific responsibility to address this issue and to build a recognized, national training pathway that those individuals who were part of the existing or future children's or adults' services work-force could engage with in order to specialize in parenting support. This pathway would take account of what was already in existence and draw the various elements together into a coherent progression route that would need the support of all stakeholders to promote and embed as part of a national workforce reform agenda. By 2010 some progress had been made, but there was still no recognized specific qualification route for parenting practitioners. Each local authority had funding to employ two senior parenting practitioners to take forward the agenda in relation to parenting education and staff development as part of the delivery of parenting strategies.

What qualities do parenting practitioners need?

Time and time again research into the characteristics of effective parenting practitioners emphasizes the significance not just of what they know, but of how they behave (Barrett 2003; Grimshaw and McGuire 1998; Smith 1996). Empathy, warmth, understanding, respect and a non-judgemental approach are needed alongside a sense of compassion. But they also require persistence, the ability to convey, in thought, word and deed, that they are there for the long haul, that the parents they are working with matter enough to experience an investment in the relationship which reflects how important not only their children are, but they are too.

Are you surprised that a specific training pathway did not exist for parenting practitioners at this time? Can you envisage any risks in professionalizing parenting support by creating roles with a perceived specific expertise in supporting parents? In your view, are there any risks in not doing so?

The characteristics of the effective parenting practitioner were becoming increasingly clear at the turn of the twenty-first century. They needed to have a very sound understanding of child development. They required not only knowledge about the range of agencies available to support the wider family agenda but also to be comfortable and respectful of the various skills and knowledge that lay in these different agencies. It was crucial that they had the necessary abilities to build trusting, open and transparent relationships with these different agencies and would share information with them.

Effective parenting practitioners need to be able to engage with adults as parents and therefore as clients of children's services and not just of adults' services. They need to recognize that many of the behaviours for which the adult might be receiving support: dangerous drug or alcohol use, mental health problems, antisocial or criminal behaviour, domestic violence, disability, family breakdown, are also affecting those adults' parenting capacity. This is likely to be reflected in their children's behaviour, school attendance, emotional well-being and educational attainment, but will not necessarily be addressed in a fully joined-up way with the family as a whole or by directly addressing the need for developing effective parenting skills through robust, readily available and embedded parenting education and support.

In fact, parenting support activities as defined above were often available only through short-term grants or where individual practitioners chose to build this into their existing day jobs on a fairly ad hoc basis. The picture was of parenting education and support being uncoordinated, ill defined and patchy even though parents were viewed as so significant to outcomes for children. In the UK, once children reached school age, parenting support from practitioners was primarily targeted at those parents with children deemed to be at risk of poor outcomes or where there was a recognized 'symptom' of a parenting 'problem': low attainment, poor school attendance, antisocial behaviour, self harm. Even though parenting was known and recognized to be challenging, parenting support was not viewed as an entitlement or as an essential part of how a community chose to organize its responsibilities to itself. We might have said, 'It takes a whole village to bring up a child', but were we behaving in ways that showed we really meant that? Where there were clear issues of neglect, services could intervene but without those indicators, with different perceptions of thresholds for need and finite resources, a range of judgements came into play about when to act in relation to parenting issues and whose responsibility it was to do so.

> What do you feel about the characteristics for effective parenting practitioners outlined above? Do you feel these are what they would need to demonstrate or are there other sets of knowledge, skills or values you would expect them to hold? Do some people have these naturally, or could they be developed through training? Should they be?

The role of parenting programmes

The experience of passing parenting skills and expertise from one generation or parent to another has a tradition that can be traced back for thousands of years in different cultures. However, delivering formalized parenting programmes that involve a group of parents coming together to learn systematically parenting skills from pre-produced, written materials with government funding that go beyond those associated with pregnancy, delivery and breast feeding have a tradition stretching back only into the late part of the twentieth century.

Before then parenting behaviours, hints and tips about how to understand and conduct the parent–child relationship were learnt either from trial and error or from watching and interacting with other older family members who generally lived close by. As the way that families organize themselves changes, the traditional networks of support from relatives often become fractured. As a consequence some families become isolated, not knowing where to turn for that practical, intergenerational support for bringing up children on which they might have relied in the past.

This becomes potentially more challenging as the situation moves generation by generation and families become further removed from any models for a 'shape' for family life to which to refer. Families increasingly come in very many different shapes and sizes and there are an increasing number of 'templates' on offer. Traditional roles have changed so much that people are able to conduct family life in a wide variety of ways.

> How would you describe a family? What might it consist of? What range of people could be taking on the role of 'parent' and how might they vary in terms of their age, biological relationship to the child, gender, role and place of habitation from, say, a hundred years ago? What impact might this variety of ways of conducting family life have on parenting?

In the western world there was a rapid increase during this period in the range and quality of parenting programmes that were designed to be accessed in different community settings. Many of these programmes were developed in response to specific needs and were generally delivered on a weekly basis by individuals with a very wide range of skills and abilities. Some of the programmes were described as 'evidence based' and had the benefit of extensive randomized controlled evaluation, close supervision and support for the facilitators and longitudinal assessment of their impact on outcomes for children. But the vast majority of parenting programmes available during this period relied on informal feedback, and were able to be delivered only where funding and enthusiasm would allow.

As a result, although the programmes were generally popular and could be shown to various degrees of reliability to be effective in changing behaviour and improving the skills and confidence of both children and parents, they were not embedded into communities in any reliable or sustainable way, nor did their delivery constitute part of the 'day job' of most professionals. Service managers and head teachers, while recognizing that parenting was crucial, did not always find it easy to make connections between their staff intensively delivering parenting programmes to 'their' parents and the targets that their services had to achieve.

What do you feel about providing parenting support through systematically delivering parenting programmes that effectively 'teach' parenting skills? Could this make the difference to outcomes for children or make parents feel judged? What do you think would be more important – the quality of the programme or the attitude and skills of the facilitator? Can you explain your reasons for your views?

Does the lack of systematic, sustainable access to parenting programmes matter in a discussion about parenting support? If we accept the premise that parenting is challenging and that support, for anyone, is helpful from time to time then the fact that traditional family members and mentors were often not as evident, or if they were then their views were based on a 'traditional' parenting situation that no longer existed, could mean that the quality of parenting, and therefore outcomes for children, were more vulnerable.

Moving parenting support away from the informal, tried and tested, trial and error approach associated with hints and tips being handed down through families into a far more professionalized context involving 'specialists' could also be problematic.

What tensions can you identify that could result from increasingly 'professionalizing' parenting support by establishing specialist parenting practitioners and what pressures might this bring to bear on those trying to deliver the parenting role? What benefits might it also bring to improving parents' knowledge and skills in relation to children's development? What criteria should be used to identify these parenting specialists and would they have to be paid professionals, recognized experienced members of a community or is there room for both?

When parenting support was delivered primarily informally and within families, it was likely that everyone involved with the family would have an ongoing relationship with each other. Without individuals who knew about the history of the child and the family, parents would need to keep having to retell their stories to different people who passed in and out of their lives and the lives of their children. It could be more difficult for those that they turned to for support to see either their behaviour or their children's in any historical context.

Here is an example of where this could be problematic for professionals who work with families for only a short time: I began working with a mother with three-year-old twins who were about to go to nursery. They had been born very prematurely and were making, to me at least, excellent progress. Like a number of other professionals involved with the family, I was struggling to understand their mother's nervousness about them starting at a nursery school, very close to their home, where they would receive lots of support from very professional staff even though their needs for extra help were minimal.

It was only when she showed me the three-year-old pictures of them as tiny newborn babies in the intensive care unit, surrounded by medical equipment, ventilators and drugs, that I started to understand her 'over-protectiveness'. 'I'm not a fussy mum,' she said. 'It's just that although these were taken three years ago, that seems like only yesterday to me.' I suddenly had an insight into the impact that those events had made on her life and that of the rest of the family in a way that only those who had lived through them really ever could.

What other sorts of situations might families have lived through that it would be very difficult for an outsider to understand but that could have an impact on their expectations for the outcomes for their children and the type of support they wanted them to have? What are the implications of this for the way we organize our services and for professionals who offer parenting advice and are seeking to tailor this to individual circumstances in order for it to be taken on board and effective?

What do parenting programmes do?

Parenting programmes delivered to groups of mothers, fathers and/or carers are, at their best, times and spaces where parents can focus and reflect on their parenting experiences. Answers to challenging behaviours and situations are often offered by other 'experts' – parents and carers in the group. Sometimes the advice goes straight to the heart of the problem, when there is a really close or 'best fit' between the needs expressed and the intervention suggested and undertaken. In my experience, these are the times when real listening has occurred, when the person offering the support has taken on board the full constellation of needs and circumstances of the parenting situation and tailored the advice to meet it. The situation has been assessed and collectively those involved have decided on the best course of action for them as a family.

Here is an example that illustrates some of these features: as part of the delivery of a parenting programme, I met a mother of three little boys and the class teacher for the eldest, who was six years old. The teacher had asked to meet with the mother because she was concerned about the boy's slow progress in developing reading skills. At nearly six years old he could not confidently find the front or back of a book, barely recognized any letters and was only vaguely aware that words and pictures could relate to each other. The teacher suggested a bedtime routine with a short story each night and went to get some suitable reading material. When she left the room, the mother looked distraught:

> I know what she wants. She wants me to have a nice cuddle with him, everything to be quiet and peaceful – bit like an advert. It's not like that in our house. By the time it gets to bedtime I'm so shattered I just want the boys in bed – I'm in no mood for a read!

She talked me through her day. Having three children all fairly close in age was tough and physically demanding, but she did manage to get them all in the bath every night: 'That's their play time,' she said. 'My partner takes the baby off to get him ready for bed and the older two have a splash time for a bit.' 'Have you ever tried bath books?' I asked. 'You can get some good ones that you could use to teach how to find the words and turn the pages and make it part of the fun.' She looked amazed. 'Would that count as reading?' she asked. Suddenly we had found a way together of establishing support that would enable her child's literacy to develop in a way that was manageable for her to deliver.

Parenting programmes with robust evaluations tend to follow closely a set programme. The programme facilitators are carefully trained to do this, but need to look for opportunities to individualize the support to specific circumstances of the parents as well. Tailoring support to the day-to-day real existence of parents rather than offering off-the-shelf ideas that do not fit with the lifestyles or circumstances of a family is critical to the take up and impact of that support. It is important that we are offering support that is solution focused rather than problem focused, that acknowledges how far we have come rather than how far we have still got to go, recognizes even the smallest steps taken but is persistent in the face of negativity and demonstrates that we are not giving up. This all serves to show to the parent that their parenting situation matters, and so do their children.

Could a poorly delivered parenting programme or other parenting support intervention, no matter how well intentioned, do more than harm than good? How would providing follow-up individualized 'wrap around' parenting support at home enable parents to take the information learnt during the programme session and make it applicable to the specific home circumstances?

Who are parenting programmes for?

Parenting programmes, in theory at least, could be available, accessible and potentially useful to any parent, regardless of their parenting situation. In practice the latter part of the twentieth and early twenty-first centuries saw parenting programmes being delivered as part of a set of services available on a voluntary basis in local communities, and hence accessed by parents with a very wide range of needs. Or they were offered as part of some kind of statutory order or contract tied in to a set of sanctions which the parents would experience if they did not attend. These could include fines, sentencing or even the taking of their children into care.

Where parenting programmes were delivered on a voluntary

basis, they were frequently targeted at parents in situations known to bring particular risk to outcomes for children but not always accessed by them without significant engagement and confidence building work. These vulnerable parents included teenagers, parents with drug and alcohol issues, mental health problems, disabilities in themselves or their children, refugees and asylum seekers, parents living in temporary accommodation or homeless, parents experiencing domestic violence. These parents would sometimes express the view that they were not supported particularly consistently or that services could be better coordinated before their situations had become highly problematic and the interventions required were far more resource intensive, expensive and often needed longer to effect change.

What do you feel about seeking to target parenting support earlier to those parenting situations that statistically have been shown to be more likely to lead to poor outcomes for children? Why do you think parents in these situations often needed a lot of relationship-building work to be undertaken before they would come into a parenting programme? How would you measure the impact of such early intervention? What would count as a 'success'? What about the idea that *all* parents could benefit from accessing a parenting programme?

Parent Early Intervention Project (PEIP)

In 2008 the government made specific funding available to parenting commissioners in local authorities through what was known as the Think Family grant to deliver evidence-based parenting programmes to targeted families with children aged between 8 and 13 years. The funding was to be used to train staff in one or more of a small number of identified parenting programmes which were chosen because of the evaluations that had been carried out into their efficacy.

The National Academy for Parenting Practitioners (NAPP) oversaw the roll out of the training of trainers and then in turn local authorities were required to ensure that those trained individuals delivered the parenting programmes to identified parents that met the targeted criteria. This work was called the Parent Early Intervention Project (PEIP).

The University of Warwick was responsible for the evaluation of the impact of PEIP and published several reports about it (e.g. Lindsay et al. 2008). In general the reports found that the evidence-based programmes are effective and it does not really matter which ones are used. The skills of the facilitators are critical to the engagement of the parents, the wrap-around support is crucial for sustaining engagement and the programmes are most effective if part of a family and parenting support package tailored to individual needs. There are difficulties in sustaining the engagement of practitioners in delivery of programmes once they have been trained. Managers do not always find it easy to build the delivery of parenting programmes into their staff's day jobs, even though this could enable them to meet 'their' targets in relation to areas such as attendance at school or attainment or behaviour. Work is needed on national indicators and the development of recognition of the role of parenting programmes and parenting support in meeting these.

Are you surprised that it is so difficult for practitioners to include the delivery of parenting programmes into their day jobs, even though they are shown to be so effective in outcomes for children? What do you think might have been some of the barriers to ensuring that this happened and what information do you think would help to change these perceptions?

The role of the facilitator

It is pointless for parenting programmes to be available in the community if parents do not access them. A whole host of barriers can be encountered: lack of publicity, misplaced perceptions about what the programme is for and who it is aimed at, fear of being judged or told off, lack of an infrastructure such as childcare or transport to support attendance, local feedback and perception about the value of attending. Facilitators are crucial to these messages and, together with other parents, the main source of transmitting them throughout a community.

How easy is it for 'support' to come across as criticism? Does it matter who the person is that is offering the support and what their role is in relation to the parent? How aware are people offering support of the impact of their power – perceived or otherwise – on a parent's attitude towards them? Could some parents be nervous about asking for support because they are afraid that they will be judged to be unfit parents?

Training for parenting practitioners

Much has been written about the knowledge, skills and values needed by those that facilitate parenting support. The National Academy of Parenting Practitioners began developing a training pathway for these individuals to follow and to be embedded into the career path of practitioners delivering parenting support as a part of or all their role from initial professional qualification stage and beyond. The development in 2005 of National Occupational Standards relating to parenting practitioners had taken this identification of a specific skill set even further but parenting practitioner was not a recognized profession in its own right (Parenting UK 2010). The early part of the twenty-first century saw a significant increase in the focus on developing the knowledge and skills of parenting practitioners through the work of the parenting commissioners and the taking forward of a workforce reform agenda for these individuals by the NAPP and later the Children's Workforce Development Council (CWDC). Time will tell the extent to which parenting support, much like educational psychology or speech and language therapy, will eventually become a service in its own right.

What would you look for in someone who was going to provide parenting support? How would it need to be differentiated depending on their role? What knowledge would you expect them to have? What skills? What values and experiences? Would they need to be a parent? Would it matter if they were a mother or a father figure?

Effective facilitators of parenting programmes generally are seen to need excellent knowledge about children's development, strong skills in facilitating adult learning, very good communication skills and the ability to assess needs and identify appropriate resources to meet these. They need the ability not only to be empathic but also to challenge without being judgemental and to be able to adopt a solution-focused approach to the work that they do that recognizes strengths and builds on the positives.

To do this effectively requires practitioners providing parenting support – who could come from a range of professional backgrounds – to be persistent, accessible locally and to have a long-standing, open and honest relationship with the family. Having access to the type of therapeutic supervision for the work that they are doing that could sensibly and intelligently challenge their own practice really helps. They need to be able to recognize when they are becoming too close to a family's issues and unable to be objective. Fundamentally it is important for them to believe that all parents have abilities and capacities to bring up their children and are entitled to be able to access the support to unleash these in the communities where they live.

> When might it be useful to have an outsider's perspective on a parenting situation? When could it be unhelpful? How important do you feel it is to blend objective and subjective assessments of parenting situations? What would you view as being the principal goal of effective supervision in such circumstances?

Other types of parenting support

Not all the signs of problematic behaviour developing are obvious when we are in a situation. They have a way of creeping up on us without us noticing. Parents will sometimes comment on the fact that it was only when a family member, friend or professional brought an aspect of their child's or their parenting behaviour to their attention that they became aware of the possible longer-term impact of what they were doing. Even then we all generally need support to enable us to change any long-standing behaviour or habit.

This can be at the level of being given factual information. I am reminded of the pregnant woman who carefully blew her cigarette smoke out of the window to avoid damaging the health of her toddler, but had to be told of the impact of her smoking on her unborn child. Or it could be something more psychological: children who grow up constantly criticized are known to develop low self esteem. Drawing attention to a child's faults without rewarding any of their positive features or just dismissing them will do this. It's not always easy for those of us who are parents to stand back from such behaviour and recognize that this is what we are doing. Parenting support can exist at the level of befriending, signposting and sharing long before it gets to the point of addressing issues through parenting programmes.

Signposting, scaffolding, supporting, safeguarding and celebrating

There is more on this in Chapter 8, but there is plenty of evidence that whatever the task, people need encouragement and positive feedback to keep going. That feedback needs to be consistent, immediate, tailored to our individual needs and delivered in ways that convey sincerity and authenticity.

With any role, but particularly one like parenting that will last a lifetime, it is easy to lose confidence. The ride is never straightforward, there will be good times and bad ones and parents will, at times, feel elated and at others desperate.

Parents, and particularly mothers, have been shown to be extremely appreciative in what they have to say about those individuals, be they family members, friends or professionals, who give such support. 'I don't know what I would have done without him/her', 'She saved my life', 'The one person that believed we could do it.' Being believed in and challenging those inner voices that might be saying 'I can't do this' can be enormously helpful and encouraging, particularly if that encouragement goes hand in hand with practical help.

That practical help can cover factual information about where support can be obtained – *signposting* – but needs to exist alongside a step-by-step approach to how to access that – *scaffolding*. This is primarily where a larger step is broken down into its smaller components and an individualized plan to enable those involved to move gradually from one point to the next is developed and implemented.

As parents, we have a responsibility to give appropriately positive messages to our children, so it is useful if we learn to give them to and receive them for ourselves. Sadly, many parents have little access to systematic positive feedback about their parenting and find themselves only accessing support when their relationship with their child has deteriorated significantly or to the point where the authorities:

the police, social services, schools, other relatives or authority figures within a family or community, are expressing concern about some element of their behaviour. It is hardly surprising that parents feel judged at this point, scared of losing their children and reluctant to ask for help. I am reminded of the single father of four young children bitterly resenting the fact that the children of the local, married GP were always turning up in school scruffily dressed. 'No one would dream of criticizing her as a mother,' he said 'but if my kids came to school looking like that, someone would be sharp at my door.'

> Are decisions on who needs advice on parenting based on judgements made by others arising from stereotypes or are some parenting situations more risky and likely to lead to poor outcomes for children than others? To what extent do you think parenting support could reinforce the resilience of families to deal effectively with the difficulties they may face?

Who is parenting support for?

Like most things, when it comes to parenting support, one size does not fit all. Some situations are tougher than others to live in. If, on top of all the other challenges, we put parenting into the scenario it is likely to be even tougher still. The relationship between parents and children has the potential to enhance and enrich everyone involved, what Bettelheim (1987) described as the chance to 'explore, relive and resolve', to be enormously rewarding, great fun and hugely fulfilling. It may be the only job a person undertakes but it is arguably the most important.

> Is it in society's interests to support parents in their parenting? How effectively and consistently do you feel we are doing so currently? What would improve the situation?

It is important that the support offered to parents is realistic and based on what is really known about the parenting situation. Parents are probably well used to having information about their child that says 'this is what they are doing now, this is what they are capable of achieving' without this necessarily going hand in hand with information about how to get from A to B. Does it matter if what the child is thought to be capable of achieving is not the same as the boy or girl next door, their brother or sister, if it's their personal best?

Challenge, responsibilities, hard work and persistence, consequences

Parents will often comment on the degree to which they have been taken by surprise by the level of demands placed upon them by the parenting role and the challenge of considering the needs of another human being above their own. Is it good enough as a parent to settle for anything less than one's best commitment to supporting a child which will almost certainly mean needing to plan life differently to help to achieve that? Are professionals consistently fulfilling responsibilities to develop ways to support parents to do this? As a society are we always meeting our responsibilities to prioritize and direct the resources needed to achieve this and how will we know that we are making a positive difference to outcomes for children as a result?

Providing parenting support in partnership with adults' services

Where parents have the kinds of issues that are either not going to go away or will need lengthy interventions such as a disability, mental health issues, drug or alcohol dependencies, this type of long-standing support for parenting becomes even more significant. Building coherent, joined-up integrated provision for families across children's and adults' services began to be a key focus in terms of government policy and practice in the early part of the twenty-first century and led to the development of such initiatives as:

- Family Pathfinders (bringing children's and adults' services together to work intensively with identified families: see DCSF 2010c).
- The Common Assessment Framework (a tool for sharing perceptions about the assessed needs of a family: see DCSF 2009a).
- Lead professionals (individuals charged with acting as the

coordinators and main points of contact for families being supported by a range of agencies: see DCSF 2010d).

- ContactPoint (the database on which all information about the range of professionals working with any child was to be logged: see DCSF 2009b).
- Family Intervention Projects that challenged and supported some of the most vulnerable families with very high levels of antisocial and problematic or high risk behaviour and supported the development of parenting skills as part of that intervention. There was growing evidence at the time, particularly from the work of FIPs, of the impact of these targeted, persistent, tenacious and highly coordinated services on the outcomes for families at risk.

Challenge and support for parenting

It could be argued that we give mixed messages about parenting. In trying, through our attempts to accommodate, to support and be understanding of the difficulties that can be associated with the role, individuals may sometimes overlook or be less demanding about the responsibilities and challenges that come with it. At the same time, when faced with children demonstrating very poor outcomes: at risk of harm, poorly educated, behaving in ways that demonstrate lack of concern for anyone than themselves, then it is the parenting behaviour that may – perhaps on occasions with some justification – be blamed. This is problematic and feels especially unfair when it is done without sufficient consideration being given to the priority that is given, or not given, to improving this and teaching better parenting skills before the situation becomes really concerning.

> Do you think we have the balance between challenging and supporting parents about right? Do we give too much attention to parents when things appear to be going 'wrong' or not enough credit when things are going 'right'?

Should we be teaching parenting skills? Do governments have a duty to support the establishment of the sorts of conditions within a society to enable parents to carry out their roles? If this has been done effectively, from where does the challenge to the parental responsibility to draw on these resources come? How do we recognize and validate the part that parents play in ensuring the best possible outcomes for their child?

In your opinion, are we making unreasonable demands on parents in society today or are we making too many excuses for them? Can you explain your answers and explore where you feel these expectations for the quality of parenting come from?

Questions to consider

- Do you feel that the job description at the start of this chapter, albeit produced in a different format from the way we might normally outline a parenting role, is a fair indication of what is involved?
- If it is, then to what extent do you feel that parents are being enabled either by society as a whole, local community-based services, friends and family or their view of themselves and their children to rise to the challenge?
- Does parenting warrant support that comes from others outside of the immediate family or is it essentially a private affair between parents and children and are we simply reverting to overly paternalistic state intervention if we provide external support?
- Are we becoming unnecessarily judgemental about the quality of the parenting that we are expecting families to provide and should society just leave parents alone to get on with the job to the best of their abilities?

5   Making change happen
Including fathers and male carers

Key themes

- Challenges of raising awareness of the specific needs of fathers and male carers in a general debate about parenting
- Role of policy and strategy in setting the legislative framework for greater father inclusion
- Turning policy into practice and changing the way services are delivered on the ground for fathers and male carers
- Applying this approach to achieving parenting support services that are more inclusive of other vulnerable or less visible parents

Focusing attention on fathers and male carers in any discussion about parental engagement is of particular significance. Fathers are not a minority group: they represent at least 50 per cent of the potential workforce.

Throughout this book the terms 'parent' and 'parenting' are used to refer to the roles of mothers, fathers and any other primary caregivers. There is still however a preponderance and greater visibility of female over male caregivers in services for parents. This chapter is a specific opportunity to consider how to address this through the engagement of fathers whom we know play a key role in outcomes for children (Goldman 2005).

In 2007 the UK government introduced the Gender Equality Duty, which required all public sector organizations to address the differing needs of men and women when developing policies and services. Despite this duty to cooperate existing in law, the extent to which changes in delivery as a result could be seen 'on the ground' in relation to men and boys in the UK was, by 2010, still patchy.

It could be argued that the process for developing policy and practice in relation to any underrepresented group is always like this.

It takes time, energy and leadership for one to be translated into the other. Policy leads the way in developing what is often a legal framework and provides the vision for where we want to get to, delivery and implementation should follow along.

History teaches us that having a legal duty is not enough on its own to make change happen. Abolishing slavery or apartheid, establishing universal suffrage and free education are all examples of policies that were enshrined in law after enormous struggles. But that was only the 'end of the beginning' in terms of establishing the change. They each became established practice through the determination of key individuals and campaigners who lobbied, challenged, fought and worked until they were fully implemented, embedded into the fabric of society and had become business as usual. Even then vigilance was still needed to continue to monitor the situation for any signs of recurring discrimination.

There will be many factors that drive such campaigns, for example a sense of injustice, a determination to advocate on behalf of a perceived underclass, a belief that some significant resource within a community is not being sufficiently harnessed and that, as a consequence, opportunities are being missed and other challenges being created that store up future problems. Very often, what begin life as 'single issue' campaigns will share underlying characteristics one with another. They almost always reflect power imbalances and inequalities of attitudes towards rights and access to resources and a perceived need to give a 'voice' to a less powerful group or underclass.

Although they may share features, each of these campaigns has a complex web of implementation issues that would benefit from specific actions. There are often subtle interplays that result from the interconnectedness of these different underlying features. Paying attention to these 'golden threads' can help to join up policy and implementation and enable us to focus on challenging inequality for one group and in doing so address a range of issues within society.

When it comes to changing practice in relation to parenting support for fathers and male carers in order to improve outcomes for children, we see why it is important to pay attention to these connections. Society becomes concerned about a particular symptom: the significant underachievement of boys in primary schools or the level of male violence would be examples, and recognizes that 'something must be done'. In developing the debate about the issue, understandings emerge about the complexity of underlying causes and a more effective strategic, coordinated response can begin to be developed. In the words of the Coalition on Men and Boys:

> Greater gender equality will reduce the pressures on men to conform to damaging and rigid forms of masculinity. This is likely to reduce men's violence, help to strengthen community safety and develop peaceful conflict resolution and improve family interaction.
>
> (Coalition on Men and Boys 2009)

A specific focus on fathers and male carers in the debate about parenting illustrates how some of these opportunities can be grasped in practice. Earlier chapters make reference to the changes that have come about in terms of roles and responsibilities in relation to family life. These have understandably had an impact on how men and women have shaped and understood their identities. This in turn has potential implications for how we set about educating boys, establish expectations about male employment and attitudes to family life, our understanding of the implications of these various challenges for men's physical and emotional well-being and our beliefs and degree of support for fatherhood.

Working this through, let's imagine that your goal is as follows:

> Dads and male carers will be as integrated and visible as mums and female carers in the service developments and activities of children's centres, extended schools and all partner organizations in your area.

How are you going to make this happen? It is highly likely that where currently parents who are raising children in situations that make the children vulnerable to poor outcomes, the fathers who are doing this are still less visible than mothers in terms of accessing the early intervention and preventative services in the community that could help them in their role.

Strategic level

Figure 5.1 identifies three different sets of change agents that generally exist in local areas and function within a social policy and political framework. At the strategic level there will often be a senior leadership

Figure 5.1   Making change happen.

team (SLT), normally a very small number of people who know they have an obligation or set of duties about father inclusion. This is likely to be only a small part of their very wide agenda but once they have a legal duty to work on this, then it is possible that they will feel a need to prioritize these responsibilities. Having these duties enshrined in law strengthens the arm of these managers to be able to argue for resources to be found to embed them. Work around father inclusion was reinforced by the introduction of the Gender Equality Duty in 2007. It is important to influence at government and ministerial level to get their commitment to a particular policy direction so that this can convert into legislation which can in turn act as a driver for change.

However, in spite of all the work that has been done nationally to establish a legal and policy context in which to undertake father inclusion work, we arguably still require a cultural shift in services to include fathers in all aspects of a child's well-being. We know this because, in spite of the legislative framework, when we ask for concrete practical examples of father inclusion work we often get a deafening silence. In that sense, having the legal framework is important but is only a step in the desired direction. Although there are pockets of good practice, in general some services for children and families were still in the early part of the twenty-first century overwhelmingly female led and not particularly father friendly.

> How visible would you say fathers are in your local antenatal, childcare or education services? To what extent would you say that families and communities behave as if when a baby is born a father as well as a mother is born? How are services supporting women to become mothers? How are they supporting men to become fathers?

If you are responsible for leading on father inclusion work in your area, you need to get the SLT to understand their obligations and to decide which bits of this policy area they want to address because, even if they wanted to, they will struggle to do it all. Tactically you are going to need to be highly strategic, determined and alert. You will have had to learn when to challenge and when to be more understanding and supportive. You will have needed to set short-term and longer-term goals and to be realistic about the pace of change. It will have been more fulfilling and more sustainable if you have built in these realistic steps otherwise you will have run the risk of becoming disillusioned, angry and burnt out. Although those of us that are impatient for change can find this highly frustrating, a more mature and effective approach to enabling change to happen is to work with senior managers rather than against them, helping them to make decisions about which bits of the agenda they can reasonably address, how they can do so and then supporting them in the process.

Managerial level

Once the strategic leads have made those decisions about priorities they need to take their service managers with them. They need these people to audit what is actually happening around father and male inclusion within their systems and develop a plan on the basis of this.

This can be tough for service managers to do. Typically they are very busy delivering to whatever targets they have been given already and dealing with all the day-to-day challenges of keeping services running to do this. From their perspective they are being battered from both sides. They have senior managers and policy makers with what (on a bad day) can seem fanciful ideas about father inclusion work, ideas that (in their view) they have no understanding of in relation to the challenges involved in turning them into practice. They have grassroots activists and clients pushing for better service delivery for them as individuals. They have regularity of reporting and accountability for the targets that they have been given the resources to manage and deliver to and responsibility for juggling ever shifting budgets to enable this to happen.

Change will happen only if these service managers are engaged. Policy and political leads and strategic managers help by creating a culture where it is safe to share what is not happening as much as what is. Changes to the rate and quality of father inclusion will not happen if audits nationally or from local areas present, for all sorts of personal and political reasons, a deceptive impression that all is well.

Open and honest debate about what is happening and why and a culture where service managers know that issues that are identified will not be dumped at their doors to solve enables this debate to move forward. Strong strategic and political support together with the willingness to free up the resources for making the changes necessary is highly important. These managers will need to know that strategic leads and politicians understand that they cannot have everything and that change takes time. If they want staff to focus on including more fathers in service provision, they will need to allow energy and resources to be directed towards that, which may well mean it needs to be directed away from something else. Strategic leads need to be absolutely convinced that this is worth doing in the long run. In other words, *they need sound evidence that the changes they are asking service managers to make will result in better outcomes for children otherwise they should not put pressure on them to make them.*

How well do you think policy makers and strategic leads research the changes they want to see happen before introducing them? How effective is the communication between them and service managers in agreeing new priorities? How does this impact on the change process?

Frontline and community levels

We have many examples in relation to working with fathers and male carers of truly innovative work happening at grassroots level. This is usually driven by passionate people, often practitioners or individuals with relevant experience on which to draw that acts as a spur to sustain their delivery.

Their work is more likely to be embedded where it is understood by strategic managers who can see the relationship between what is happening at grassroots and the heading off of bigger and longer-term issues that they have responsibility for and that are generally very costly to remediate.

At grassroots there can and will often be lots of work happening, but if it is outside the strategic political framework or not understood by those managers, it is highly vulnerable. The moment that passionate grassroots person leaves, it becomes apparent that the work is not embedded. The work may stop or dry up altogether. It might stagger on but lose dynamism, commitment or team support. The champion at grassroots level may have become famous, but their lack of succession planning and engagement needed to embed the work strategically means that those changes are not sustained. In the worst cases, because things go back to what they used to be like, people become disillusioned and cynical about the change process and the next time they are asked to change they refuse, avoid or openly resist.

Targets linked to funding can help these passionate people because they act as the bridge between the strategic and the frontline. It is a happy situation when all three are in harmony:

- The strategic direction is to engage fathers more effectively.
- There are specific targets around father engagement 'owned' by specific service managers individually and collectively.
- Resources are directed to activities at the frontline that embed the sorts of activities proven to enable those things to happen. For example, father engagement workers are employed and not only do direct work with fathers themselves but also increase the confidence of the workforce as a whole to engage fathers more effectively.

Leadership

Children's services in the early part of the twenty-first century in the UK adopted a new language. It was clear that the focus should be on *outcomes* for children and asking ourselves whether the actions we were taking, our *outputs*, were making the difference needed. Leaders were increasingly expected to gather evidence along the way to enable reflection and review of the *impact* of delivery.

We have significant research evidence that parents and parenting are crucial to outcomes for children. Fathers and male carers specifically and uniquely impact on those outcomes and the Gender Equality Duty required us to differentiate our approach to male and female caregivers. If we were not focusing on work with each of them, we were not only missing tricks but also failing in our legal responsibilities.

There was an increasing focus of attention at this time on the significance of leadership in enabling change to happen (Cabinet Office 2008). That leadership would need to be evidenced at strategic, managerial and operational levels if we were to develop and then commission services that were father inclusive. Leaders would need to be very clear about the key messages that they were seeking to convey in relation to fathers and highly skilled in presenting these in ways that would engage service managers and budget holders at national, area and local levels.

This can be a particular challenge for strategic and political leaders who may find themselves held responsible for addressing a particular behaviour that is concerning the public, having to spend time understanding the factors that contribute to this behaviour while simultaneously needing to be seen to be doing something fairly quickly and pragmatically to address it. Politicians are not always helped in this by a public hungry for things to be fixed, an impatient media able to draw attention to examples of ongoing perceived failures, our competitive system of election and still relatively few examples of power sharing and cross-party debate about what causes social issues.

Learning how to harness these public perceptions and priorities in order to direct resources to them is a key skill for leaders. Gladwell (2000) describes the process whereby public opinion and understandings develop to a stage where eventually attention is sufficiently focused on an issue and informed about it for consistent and effective action to be taken.

Is it important to have fathers visible in their own right in services for parents? How could we better present the reasons for this? To what extent do we need to be aware of timing, choice of language, harnessing the passion without turning that into pedantry? How can leaders be both persistent and tenacious and balance challenge with support?

How can those who are trying to lead the change demonstrate patience in the face of what will often be a slow-moving agenda? To what extent should they be acknowledging and rewarding small steps towards goals and providing the scaffolding needed to enable each move and on the other hand driving the change and challenging the status quo?

In summary, we need leaders who can communicate clearly, skilfully and respectfully, use whatever platforms are available to them at strategic, managerial or grassroots levels and use champions effectively at each level and sustain their authenticity so they are trusted and viewed as doing all this for the right reasons – to improve outcomes for children. They need to have governance arrangements in place for fathers and father champions to enable them to influence how services are shaped in the future, to identify and support good practice and to challenge complacency.

Despite the difficulties, there is a sense in which there is no choice but to promote father-inclusive services: fathers are just too important for the outcomes for children not to do so. Leadership teams could adopt a position statement about fathers and male carers' inclusion. The National Services Framework allows for this by setting standards for children's health and social services and explains the relationship between those services and children's education. They could make it a requirement that any agency that they commission services from for parents has signed up to that statement about father inclusion and can demonstrate how they are meeting it, much as they would expect them to have a policy and set of procedures in relation to safeguarding.

Workstreams to deliver father and male inclusion as part of parenting support

In my experience, when seeking to establish new ways of working, leaders need to have an eye to three parallel workstreams.

Workstream 1: service delivery

Never underestimate the power of establishing good practice examples that model effective father and male carer inclusion and demonstrate a fully working service delivery model that managers and strategic leads can see. Make sure that these examples are not hidden away, celebrate and promote them, encourage those involved to share their stories and publish what works and why.

At the same time, work hard not to oversell a model without explaining all the complexities and efforts that have been invested to achieve the quality of delivery that has been established. Be aware that hard-pressed managers, politicians and strategic and policy leads can sometimes miss the complexities, infrastructure and coordination involved to achieve this success unless these are fully explained.

Capture the story as you develop these services as you go along and document their development. Investment in evaluation and research, training and mentoring all enable these practices to become understood and help them to be embedded. It is well worth engaging a critical friend or action researcher or evaluator to work alongside you to enable the reflective practice to develop along the way and to build this into service delivery so that you have a model for continuous improvement arising from a plan, do, review cycle that is informed regularly by feedback from service users and not yet reached potential service users.

Workstream 2: workforce reform and training

Having staff that truly buy into and commit to providing a quality service delivery where men and women each experience fully inclusive practice will inevitably make the difference between a 'good enough' and an exceptional parenting provision.

How visible are men and images of family life in the documentation that you encounter? What messages does this convey to staff about the importance of including fathers?

There were a number of examples of such practice around the UK in the early part of the twenty-first century and these were showcased in documentation from the Fatherhood Institute and the DCSF.

Sadly all too often it is a child's death at the hands of a father or male carer that draws media attention to the knowledge, skills and experiences that many staff have in engaging with these parents, or recognizing and being able to address warning signs of stress and dangerous practice in their parenting skills. In some serious case reviews after such tragedies, a picture has emerged that suggests that if workers are engaging with the mother, they sometimes behave as if by doing so they are engaging with the family as a whole. As a result they may be addressing the mother's personal and parenting needs more effectively than those of the father who is, in effect, invisible to the practitioners.

The workforce agenda needs to reinforce images of men as part of families to enhance their visibility and prompt practitioners to ask about them. Case studies need to include fathers and family men with practitioners being invited to share what definition of family they are working to. If we do not have fathers and family men visible in the culture of our services, how can we expect the workforce to work with them? Male as well as female carers should be reflected in all images of families that services use and position statements endorsed by the senior leadership team. We need to continue to do more to reinforce the visibility of men in the children's workforce generally so as to promote the notion that men can have a positive role in children's lives.

Workstream 3: performance management

It is extremely difficult to identify cause-and-effect relationships in social policy and one can feel a very long way from the other. This makes it difficult to sustain commitment across the various parts of the system to father engagement. Having both quantitative and qualitative data to inform how resources can be most effectively deployed, where they have the greatest impact and how they can best be used to head off the need for more costly interventions in the future is critical.

> Whatever the level of resource we have access to, even if it is only our own individual time and energies, to what extent do you feel that we each have stewardship over those resources, are responsible and ultimately accountable for the choices we make in relation to how we use them? How could we reinforce that sense of accountability?

In 2009 the Fatherhood Institute produced a Dad Test Guide and Logbook, as part of the DCSF-backed Think Fathers campaign 'to ensure health, education and other local services are targeted at both parents to offer the best possible support for children and their families' (Fatherhood Institute 2009). It was hoped that it would help all health, family and children's services, schools and third sector agencies to identify how they could engage more effectively with fathers by identifying not only good practice but also areas for further work.

Do auditing tools like this have their place? Can they raise anxiety by creating awareness of issues if they do not provide the necessary scaffolding to enable change to happen? Are they a useful way of getting 'buy-in' to the change process by allowing people to feel more in control by doing a self evaluation and coming to an awareness of their point on the journey and a desire to take the next steps at their own pace?

When incorporating and endorsing such opportunities for self evaluation the senior leadership team is giving permissions to managers to challenge their practice, identify strengths and areas for improvement with a view to addressing these. They will obviously need to give them time, space, resources to make these adjustments. That kind of permission has to permeate all the way through an organization and demonstrate very clearly that the SLT is serious about commissioning and decommissioning services based on a shared set of criteria and values and will not be satisfied, for example, with data that shows that 'parents' are being reached but is not expecting data that differentiates between mothers and fathers.

Developing fully inclusive, integrated early intervention parenting support services for all

Creating parenting support that is inclusive of fathers and mothers is critical for effective outcomes for children. However, the models for effective working across strategic, managerial and frontline delivery outlined here could be applied to any targeted group that we know faces challenges that impact on their parenting capacity, such as grandparents, teenage parents, parents with children with disabilities, as well as parents with their own personal challenges, for instance mental health issues, substance misuse problems, personal disabilities, refugee and asylum seeker status, members of black and minority ethnic communities who may be feeling excluded as well as anyone attempting to parent against a backdrop of poverty.

Research evidence tells us where the likely impact on outcomes for children will occur if we do not support these parenting situations. Our challenge is can we afford not to do so?

Questions to consider

- Very often like-minded individuals will form local or national networks to try to promote father inclusion. How can those networks serve to bring the voice of fathers themselves into the debate at a strategic level and what techniques are available to them to do so?
- How can leaders balance gaining the commitment and trust of mainstream agencies with maintaining the integrity and challenge that grassroots organizations need to advocate on behalf of fathers (or indeed any other currently under-represented group)?
- How might we succeed in translating what can be viewed as being an intensely personal view of fatherhood and male inclusion that maintains its cutting edge and clarity into an approach accepted by the mainstream as just 'the way we do things around here'?
- What can we learn from making change happen in relation to making services more father friendly that we could apply to other underrepresented groups of parents?

6 Nurturing parents as people

Key themes
- The emotional energy required to parent effectively
- Recognizing and reinforcing that parents have other identities
- Balancing and prioritizing the needs of parents with the responsibilities parents have to children
- Some of the potential consequences of failing to nurture

This chapter is about the nurture and support that parents need in order to be at a point where they are able, in turn, to nurture and support their children.

> Parenting effectively can be emotionally draining. Where do parents develop the resilience and emotional reserves to draw on, particularly when parenting gets tough? To what extent does this resilience depend on:
> - the practical support that they can access
> - their personal value base
> - their physical and emotional well-being?

Very little prepares a person for the impact that having a child can have. Becoming a parent is accompanied not only by profound physical changes in the case of mothers but also significant emotional and psychological changes in fathers and mothers. Even the best prepared or the most physically distant or emotionally absent parent will experience some disruption and upheaval when a baby is born.

In modern societies, becoming a parent brings legal, social and financial responsibilities that can, and often will, be enforced if they are not embraced willingly by the individuals involved. These responsibilities are significant ones that take time and energy to fulfil. Parents draw on their physical and emotional reserves to meet them and, when their own reserves run dry, will often need to draw on others around them until they are replenished.

Not all parents are fortunate enough to have such support or find themselves taken by surprise by the impact of these additional responsibilities and can, often very quickly, find themselves physically exhausted and emotionally rung out. This is not good for them and, in turn, not ideal for their children.

The parenting journey: myths and realities

There are a number of ways that parents are alerted to the nature of the journey they are undertaking. These messages are all around us about what parenting is like, but in many ways they are quite confused and confusing. Images of happy families and contented babies are regularly reinforced in advertising of products for children and parents. Such images may not always equate with an individual's reality of caring for a child. Even where individuals have had first-hand experience before becoming a parent themselves, there are still adjustments to be made to becoming the person with a relationship for life with another human being.

- Which images of what parenting is like do you see portrayed in advertising?
- Why do you think parenting is portrayed in these ways?
- How far do you feel these images reflect the reality of parenting and what gives you this perspective?
- What impact, if any, do you feel these images may have on our impression of what being a parent is like?

Parents may be surprised by the gap between the images of parenting and the realities they experience and can have various reactions to these. For some, the images provide a target that they can never hope to achieve and they will give up immediately or make unrealistic demands on themselves and their children to achieve that perceived ideal. Some will embrace the change and adapt, others may try to ignore the additional demands and carry on much as before, relying on others to make adjustments to accommodate to the demands of parenthood.

Effective parenting requires in part the ability to hear, interpret and respond appropriately or 'tune in' to a child's needs. Parents that make only minimum attempts to do this tuning in and responding to their child's needs generally fail to be as adequate or effective as they might be. This will, in all probability, result in poorer outcomes for that child, depending on the other conditions that exist in the child's wider environment and also the traits and capabilities inherent within that individual child. As has been rehearsed earlier, while a parent's behaviour matters, it has a role only in shaping a child's destiny, not in fully controlling it.

- • What factors might inhibit a parent's ability to 'tune in' to their child's needs?
- • Could some of these factors be temporary or long-standing?
- • Could they relate to factors in the parent or the child or the family or the community?
- • What might help to reduce the impact of these factors?

Living in the moment

Being alive to the opportunities and possibilities in a relationship is one thing. Enjoying that relationship in the here and now, with all its idiosyncrasies, is another. One of the problems of focusing on outcomes for children is that it can encourage us to be so future orientated that we fail to be fully present in the here and now. Instead we are investing now for a future return, not for an enjoyment and acceptance of the age and stage we are living in with our child at present.

Some parents love the stage when their children were dependent on them for their basic care, others cannot wait for that stage to be over so their child can be more independent. Some of this is to be expected and reflects where parents feel more confident in their own abilities. But we perhaps need to be alive to the fact that society, parents and children themselves can often be responsible for raising the bar on behaviour expectations in the present because they are in a hurry to get to a place in the future, for example where children are independent financially, secure and in a positive relationship. Or parents may want to hang on to a place in the past where they felt happiest and most secure, which for some parents could be when their child was too young to make independent decisions. We shall return to this topic in Chapters 7 and 8, and explore the relationship between our view of what parenting is for and the significance of loving and accepting our children for who they are, even though we may not always like what they do.

Enabling parenting behaviour that achieves the best outcomes for children

It is very tempting to try to identify factors in a child's upbringing that, if reinforced, would support their development. Do you think it is possible to identify and isolate any factors that make for effective parenting? By addressing those factors consistently, would we be able to guarantee better outcomes for children? In doing this, how important would simply spending time with and enjoying the parent–child relationship emerge as a factor in those outcomes?

One of the most difficult aspects of studying any form of social behaviour is to isolate factors and influences in the environment and be confident that we have controlled their impact. Parenting does not take place in laboratory conditions where we can match specimens, control all aspects of the environment, or isolate particular inputs to compare and contrast their impact on outcomes.

As a consequence, there is no clear cause-and-effect relationship that has been consistently proven to exist between a particular parenting situation and outcomes for children. However, we know that some situations can make life more challenging generally, and as a consequence can be expected to impact also on parenting capacity and the ability to tune in to a child's needs. We know that there are a number of parenting situations that contribute to this ability. Many of these situations reflect issues in the environment such as poverty and availability of resources, education and health. Other factors, however, are to do with the innate traits and personalities of not only the child but also the parents themselves and the choices that they make in relation to their child.

Risk factors in parenting

Where a parent is very immature, or has had a history of poor parenting themselves, or is irresponsible about their personal health and safety – misusing drugs or alcohol for instance – or is emotionally distant or financially unstable, or is living without the support of family or friends, or is experiencing relationships that are dangerous or violent, then there is statistically less likelihood that they will be able to parent effectively.

There are no guarantees that this will be the case because some individuals can and do overcome enormous problems and disadvantages, either alone or, more often, with the support of others. However, such situations make it difficult to care for and meet one's own needs, let alone those of a dependent child.

Can you think of any examples of parents that could be described as experiencing extremely difficult circumstances but where, in your view, there is a strong likelihood of positive outcomes for their children in spite of this? Can you also think of parents experiencing what, on the surface, could be described as a very positive set of circumstances but where you are less than optimistic about how their children will grow and develop? How significant is the quality of the parent–child relationship in making the difference in each of these scenarios?

The parent–child bond

The survival of any baby depends on their primary carers being well able to tune in to and respond to their needs. Human infants are helpless to meet their own survival needs for much longer than most other mammals and rely heavily on their parents and carers to feed, nurture and protect them. This relationship between parents and children is demanding. No matter what physical, emotional or material resources a parent may be able to draw upon to meet these demands, most will find themselves, at times, feeling that their reserves have been severely depleted, if not run dry.

As children grow up, and depending on the particular circumstances, a range of different people will contribute to their care and education. But there is a sense in which, no matter what the age and circumstances, when people become parents they are entering a relationship that is 24/7 and for life. These days we can choose to divorce ourselves from almost any other role or responsibility but with parenting even the giving up of a child totally, say through adoption, still leaves those individuals with a genetic link which, even in only a biological sense, means that the two individuals are connected.

Is it important to prepare individuals for the demands and realities of parenthood? To what extent could this be a greater focus in lessons about sex and relationships which children have at home and at school? Do we spend too much time in sex education at home or at school on the biology and not enough time on the psychology of parenting?

Human infants are equipped with a number of techniques and characteristics which enable them to bond with their main carer, draw attention to their needs and make demands on the reserves of their parents. Most obvious of these is their ability to cry in response to discomfort of any kind. There have been a number of studies into the effect of crying on mothers' response patterns to their babies' needs and the impact of mental illnesses such as postnatal depression on this and the subsequent development of the child (Kitzinger 1990).

Parents will often report on their growing ability to interpret different sorts of crying by their children – for food, for comfort, for stimulation or for tiredness – and have been shown to be able to adapt their own behaviour very effectively in response to all of these, bringing about changes in their children's levels of comfort as a result. This could be described as a parent's ability to observe, listen, tune in and then respond to their child's needs.

It takes emotional, psychological and physical energy to shut off from other distractions and do this. The younger the child, the more reliance is placed on the parents' abilities to interpret signals that are not accompanied by words. Children who are developmentally very young have only limited control of their bodies: the ability to gaze or head turn, to become still, kick and flex. Most other bodily functions and movements are involuntary so it is extremely important to very young children that their carer is listening to and interpreting their needs as expressed through some of the most basic of signals that they are making.

How much emphasis do you feel we place in our society on tuning in to the needs of children, whatever their age and however these are being communicated? How does this sometimes conflict with tuning into the needs we have as adults? How effectively are parents prepared for this potential conflict? Can it lead to them resenting the demands being a parent place on them? What impact might this have?

It has been shown that parents who are attentive to the signs and signals that their babies make can, very quickly, find themselves extremely accomplished in being able to comfort and settle that child. In itself this ability to tune in to and respond to a very young child is profoundly important for the bonding process between the parent and the infant and we know has its roots in the very earliest interactions even from before and immediately after a child's birth.

There have been a number of studies that have reinforced the significance of physical contact between parents and their infants and of practices such as swaddling babies, skin-to-skin contact, eye-to-eye contact, responding to other sounds that babies make, cooing and talking to babies for the development of emotional and physical security, language and cognition (Bowlby 1997).

But parents will also report that there are times when they are baffled by why their baby will not settle, become tired and intolerant of the constant demands that are placed on them and, much as they love their child, resent the degree by which their child has 'taken over' their lives or fails to 'appreciate' what they do for them.

When a child's needs are particularly complex or unusual, not well understood or requiring specialized input, parenting can become even more complicated and challenging. Parents with children with disabilities often describe, and understandably can often experience, a greater sense of exhaustion, isolation and frustration. They may benefit even more evidently and for longer from family support such as respite arrangements tailored to their needs.

Although some jobs are more enjoyable than others, most people have times when they would like to change something about their work or stop doing it altogether. Parenting can and should be an extremely enjoyable job, but parenting effectively involves very hard work, and is a job for life. How easy is it for parents to maintain other roles and responsibilities that they still hold, even when they have had children, and how might they be supported and prepared to make the necessary adjustments to do so?

What difference can effective nurturing make?

Studies have highlighted the impact on children of having consistently responsive care and nurturing, particularly in the early years but also at other key transition points in individual development. We are learning much more from research now, for instance, about how stress in early infancy produces chemicals that are thought to hinder the growth of the brain and the key times to take the opportunities to encourage effective stimulation and brain development. There is some evidence that while these problems can be compensated for to some extent, these missed opportunities are not able to be fully overcome later in life (Johnson 1993).

We also know more about gender differences in relation to these opportunities. There is research that suggests that missing these developmental 'windows' and creating stressed reactions in the infancy of boys has an even more profound impact on their ability to deal with stress calmly as adults than it does on girls (Bayley and Featherstone 2005).

This evidence is important to our understanding of how we can enable boys, in particular, to develop the sorts of brains and behaviours that will enable them to deal confidently and persistently with stress and challenges in the future without resorting to inappropriately aggressive or avoidance behaviours. Improving this understanding could then enable us to develop more effective approaches to reducing a number of difficulties in later life currently believed to be linked to hyperactivity and attention deficit and hyperactivity disorder (ADHD) (Timimi 2005).

These developmental windows represent what could be described as 'use it or lose it' opportunities in terms of children's brain development in their earliest years. What are the implications for how we should support, train and develop parents and carers of preschool children to tune into the needs of infants to cope with stress? In terms of heading off later problems, is there any evidence that this would be time, money and energy well spent?

'Problem' parents

Very occasionally parents are so damaged, so mentally unbalanced, so psychotic, selfish or uncaring that they simply cannot and will not protect and care for their children. Parents who demonstrate this sort of behaviour cause significant concern to societies and governments. Their children are statistically known to be vulnerable to non-attendance at school, antisocial behaviour, poor health, entering the criminal justice or care systems and unemployment.

Such behaviours are significantly damaging to these children's life chances, not to mention extremely expensive to remediate. They represent a huge waste of human potential and could be interpreted as a disturbing measure of the quality of the society in which they have grown up and its ability to care effectively for some of its most vulnerable members.

When parents behave with scant regard for their children's well-being, are they:

- just being irresponsible
- reflecting their own sense of worthlessness
- crying out for help
- doing something else?

Although there are some extreme examples of neglect, all parents experience times when the fit between their child's needs and their capacity to respond is less than perfect. At such points, parents may feel and actually do not have the physical, mental, financial or emotional resources to take on board the needs of their child. The reasons for this can be very varied and the consequences of not addressing them may have an impact that is either very short lived or, potentially, laying up longer-term and much more serious consequences.

Physical capability, health and well-being

Being unwell is obviously going to have an impact on an individual's ability to care for someone else. Adaptations can be made to a short-term, temporary illness or incapacity where a parent has some type of infrastructure in the form of family or friends on which to rely and can still impart knowledge and information about their child's needs. Long-term parental absence or physical inability to respond to a child's needs would, generally speaking in our society, lead to some more significant rethinking of the overall care for a child. For instance, we might do this by introducing some variation on a fostering or even permanent adoption arrangement.

To some extent it is easier to decide to intervene in a situation where the parenting capacity is so poor that it has clearly met a threshold whereby support is warranted because the child is at risk of significant harm. In the main, social policies and legislation reinforce the importance of sustaining the parent–child relationship in such situations and supporting the parents to develop the sorts of knowledge, skills and attitudes that would enable them eventually to care for their children effectively, whatever their age or level of need.

The safety and protection of the child is the paramount responsibility of welfare services. The UK, like other western societies, has formalized, legal procedures whereby the state has responsibilities for assessing the fit between a child's needs and the parental capacity to meet these. Ultimately welfare services have rights and responsibilities that can supersede those of parents whose care falls below a threshold that means the child is deemed to be at such risk.

The situation can sometimes be more problematic to address where parenting capacity is generally inconsistent for some reason. In practice, inconsistency is the reality for all parents who will have good days and bad days, times when they feel full of energy and times when they are too tired to really care.

In these situations it is often the debate about the threshold for the level of inconsistency in the quality of the parenting that might or should trigger an intervention which creates tensions across professionals and within families and communities. It is not uncommon for the assessment of risk to children to be very variable between different services supporting a family, the level of shared knowledge about what is happening within a family to differ and the perception of the appropriate intervention to vary widely. Time and again investigations into child deaths where parenting has been deemed neglectful; these inconsistencies, lack of coordination and poor partnership working have been highlighted. The thrust of legislation and professional development across children's services in the UK towards the end of the twentieth and early part of the twenty-first centuries was particularly designed to try to address these issues and ensure that professionals worked in a more open and consistent way to identify where parenting was problematic and, with varying degrees of success, to support effective parenting.

Although there are some behaviours that clearly do put a child at risk of significant harm, supporting parents is not an exact science. It is likely that any intervention designed to do so will, in itself, be inconsistent, affected as it will be by cultural expectations in organizations, communities and families of what constitutes good enough parenting and the available resources to support it.

> Different people have varying perspectives of which parenting behaviours constitute a risk that is of sufficient concern for children to be brought into care. We know that, statistically, children who do come into the care system often have very poor outcomes in spite of this. How should we deal with the differences in attitudes to these thresholds and to what extent do all members of a community and not just agencies like the police and social services have a duty to promote and support effective parenting?

Parenting beliefs and practices

There are places where customs and child-rearing practices have been handed down intergenerationally for many hundreds of years and continue to fit circumstances that have changed little over time. If families move or their environment is altered, perhaps by the introduction of invading populations bringing different cultures and beliefs or their own migration into different worlds, these accepted practices may be challenged.

There are numerous examples of this happening throughout

history with the subsequent impact on kinship patterns, family dynamics and sense of identity often being very keenly felt. We see the evidence of one culture swamping another in the history of European settlers overwhelming the cultures of Native Americans and the indigenous populations of countries like Australia and New Zealand. Traditional beliefs about the authority of parents over their children in black and minority ethnic cultures created considerable tensions for some children that subsequently grew up in twenty-first-century Britain. Changes in the roles and responsibilities of mothers and fathers arising from variations in the economic climate and the availability of employment has been known to lead to loss of identity and sense of place and position in a family, particularly for fathers (Crompton 1999).

These changes went hand in hand with a growing interest in and exploration of the different developmental stages that children pass through and how we might fit these into the various socially constructed steps and activities that we provide and see as relevant. The degree to which these vary from society to society and through time became increasingly apparent as we learnt more about different cultures and developed the ability to record and reflect on the growth of our own. The extent to which 'childhood' is socially constructed rather than a fixed and clearly defined period with specific requirements emerged in the latter part of the twentieth and early twenty-first centuries through much of the literature associated with childhood studies (James and Prout 1997).

> Once compulsory schooling was introduced in the UK the notion of childhood being associated with formal education began to be established. How did this impact on the attitude that society developed towards children working to support the family income and the differentiation between the responsibilities of parents and children for this?
>
> What impact might the extension of compulsory formal education have on the concept of when childhood begins and ends and how does this differ in less industrialized countries where children work from a much earlier age to earn their own living and to contribute to the family income?

Parents' ability to understand and interpret the needs of their ever-changing children will vary according to their knowledge about and understanding of children's development. Many parents comment on having confidence about how to behave at certain ages and stages of their children's lives but not at others. They receive information about how to parent from a range of different sources: other parents, professionals, the media and have to make sense of these messages. Parenting practices and advice about the best ways to care for a child can be very varied: to inoculate or not, to feed on demand or not, to pick up when crying or not, to lie the child on his or her stomach at night or not are just a few of the different behaviours that parents have to make decisions about and for which advice is not always consistent.

Personal constructs

Even with such child development knowledge, parents still need to turn thought into deed. I have described earlier how each of us carries a sense of self, of who we are and what our capabilities and futures might be. We are constantly refining these constructs in the light of our personal experiences but they are shaped by what happened in our childhood and how that interacts with our personality traits and characteristics. They reflect to some extent the degree to which we have had the opportunity to review our own behaviour and understand why we act and think as we do.

What difference do you think it could make to parents to have the opportunity to stand back from their parenting situation from time to time and gain a different perspective on it? Why do you think that so many parents who have such opportunities describe themselves as feeling relieved to discover that they were not the only people to be having challenging experiences with their children and that this was the first step towards making changes in their parenting behaviour?

We could describe this ability as being linked to increasing maturity or self awareness. There is evidence to suggest that these personal constructs and feelings about ourselves and others shape the inner conversations we have with ourselves and, in turn, the ways we interpret the behaviour of others and the actions we then take (Kelly 1963). The influence of exposure to wider cultures enables us to broaden and question these dialogues and understandings as we

encounter differences that may surprise or challenge our perceptions of what constitutes appropriate parenting behaviour. This can
reinforce messages that suggest that what is viewed as appropriate can
depend as much on the social context in which the parenting is taking place as it does on any particularly fixed view of what is 'correct'
parenting.

An example of this in relation to parenting might be our personal
constructs about what 'ideal' fathering or mothering looks like,
the degree to which parents might perceive their own fathering or
mothering matching or falling short of that and their beliefs about
the amount of responsibility they have as parents in relation to
this. Changes in economic circumstances and family dynamics alone
have meant that there have been a number of developments in attitudes towards how mothers and fathers 'should' behave over the
late twentieth and early twenty-first centuries.

> At their best, parenting programmes and parenting support provide
> spaces to focus on the implications of these changes in attitude and
> expectations for fathers and mothers and the actions needed to address
> the needs of children in spite of them. Parents often describe them-
> selves as learning new 'scripts' in these situations. What do you think
> they mean by this?

The gap between these constructs and reality will contribute to the
ways in which parents view their behaviour, their child's behaviour
and any actions that they feel they need to take in relation to these.
For example, parents with personal constructs that view mothering as
being about offering warmth, personal care and close physical contact
will feel responsible for providing these to their children and will be
uncomfortable with them not being carried out or other child carers
taking these roles. Parents who view fathering as being about setting
and reinforcing standards of behaviour could expect that behaviour
in themselves and feel guilty and that they should try harder if their
children fail to meet these standards and they are enforced elsewhere.

> Do children need fathers as well as mothers? Are there some parenting
> behaviours that only one gender should take responsibility for deliver-
> ing? Are there fundamental differences between the nurturing that

fathers and mothers provide or does it not matter where the parenting comes from as long as it is provided somewhere?

Nurturing parents as people

Parents have a job for life and one which, to do it well, requires them to be ever vigilant, constantly adapting, watching and listening not only to the behaviours of their child, but also to the actions of those around them, their peers, their siblings, their school friends, their family and community. Parents need and should be encouraged to ask for help from time to time. This is not a sign of failure. It is an indication of the sheer size of the task and the desire to do it well. What worked with one child may not work with another.

A colleague and I spent some time carrying out research that involved listening to the types of help that parents accessed for their parenting (Miller and Sambell 2003). We established that the ultimate aim of good parenting support was to enable parents to learn how to develop the efficacy of their parenting. Regardless of the parenting situation, the parents we interviewed, all mothers, asked for three broadly similar types of support as follows: dispensing support, relating support and reflecting support.

Dispensing support

In this instance parents were effectively asking 'What can I do to change my child?' and focused on the child as a problem. Support was sought from someone that the parents viewed as having expertise or 'answers'. They could be another parent, a friend or a professional, but the key was that the parent viewed the situation as requiring knowledge and facts so that was what they set out to acquire.

Relating support

In this situation the parents were typically asking how they felt about the situation in which they found themselves. They were asking this not only about their role as a parent, but also about themselves, their child and the relationship between the two. They were seeking support that focused on them as people, rather than just as parents, that made them feel respected and accepted, listened to and valued. They emerged from this kind of support not necessarily with facts or knowledge, but feeling better about themselves as human beings, comforted and nurtured.

Reflecting support

Where parents experienced this type of support they encountered individuals that enabled them to ask *why* a particular parenting scenario was taking place. They were enabled to step back from the situation as reflective practitioners and explore the relationship between themselves and their child more holistically and try to understand rather than 'solve' it.

What might we note from these findings?

Crucially, those parents who had experienced the relating model of support were the ones who appeared able to move towards taking on board this reflecting support. The non-judgemental, validating nurturing that they received from the relating support appeared to have been highly valued and important for creating a learning environment where the parents felt safe and valued. 'In turn, this allowed and legitimised parents' need to explore other possibilities within the parent–child relationship and take new meanings from these' (Miller and Sambell 2003: 41).

> Much of the research that has been carried out into the qualities of effective facilitators of parenting support has focused on the importance of nurturing parents as people by providing persistent, non-judgemental, challenging, acknowledging and respectful support. To what extent do we emphasize in parenting support services the importance of nurturing parents as people so that, in turn, they can nurture their children?

Like all human beings, parents are imperfect. That is not a problem if they focus sufficiently on the job in hand and, when it starts to go off track, do something, making it a priority to get the relationship back in line. All parents, from time to time, feel and actually are unable to cope. We should not be surprised by this. In my view, we should expect it to happen and focus on developing communities of learning where we both look out for early signs and symptoms and see it as our collective responsibility to do something about them.

It may be more difficult for parent educators to move beyond providing dispensing support through to focusing on parents as people and creating learning environments where parents feel they can reflect and ask 'why' something is 'going wrong' in their parent–child relationship. This could be because we are trying to do this against a backdrop of increasingly disconnected and fluid communities, a sense of alienation and parents (often those that need the most help) potentially hiding problems through a fear of being judged and found wanting by ever more powerful practitioners. It may also be because increasingly parents, themselves stressed and distracted, may not be recognizing problems that are developing through a lack of understanding of the parenting process or because they are so taken up with their own needs that they miss the needs of their children. It might even be that parents find themselves in a situation that is so like everyone else they know that they have lost all sense of perspective that life could actually be any different.

> Parents often complain that they have to retell their story many times to different practitioners. Would it be more helpful to families to have support tied in more closely to universal services such as schools or health or Sure Start Children's Centres so that these were more obviously hubs of activity in communities rather than referring agencies that passed families on? How would that reinforce the message that the whole 'village' was raising the child?

What worries me particularly is that, without a clear idea or memory of what confident and competent parenting looks and feels like, we will lose any sense of what it could be like. In turn, this could lead to society as a whole and the policies which successive governments introduce failing to recognize the part that they play in creating the necessary conditions in which effective parenting takes place. We could fail to take a more measured and longer-term view of where we are heading and what our collective view is of the type of society we want and how to achieve it.

If we lose a sense of a clear model or end-point of good enough parenting to tell us what we are trying to get to, we could often be wide of the mark without even realizing it.

Needing a child more than they need you

A goal of effective parenting has been said to be to have a child who grows to be their own father and mother, who can make and take responsibility for their own independent choices because they have been nurtured, enabled to stand on their own two feet and feel emotionally strong. Parents who have little access to nurturing support, positive regard and approval themselves as they raise their children may unconsciously turn to their children to give this approval and a sense of purpose to them.

> Where children act as carers for parents because of emotional, psychological or physical issues, we know there can be particular challenges relating to their own development and to the parent–child relationship. To what extent does society have a responsibility to recognize that children may be undertaking duties and responsibilities in the home more appropriate to adults and that are impinging on their own childhoods?

Where we are failing to support and nurture children by giving them confidence and security, we are contributing to a situation where they will potentially grow up to be adults who are unable to draw as effectively on emotional reserves in turn to support their children. They may inappropriately and mistakenly at times replace responding to their children's emotional needs by providing material ones, particularly if that was how they had their needs responded to as children. Material rewards can take the place of the really costly parenting demands for time, warmth and emotional attention. This is a worrying thought for the sense of belonging and well-being of those children who may be growing up in a world of increasingly fractured family life, where it is arguably even more important for parents to focus on developing in their children a sense of personal worth and belonging.

Questions to consider

- To what extent is time between parents and children to develop the bonding and relationship between them being eroded by modern living? Does this matter and, if it does, are we doing anything either within individual families, communities or through government to address the issue?
- Are we expecting other agencies or professionals to undertake too many elements of the parenting role and, if so, do we need to do anything to reinforce the quality and responsiveness of these agencies to the needs of each individual family?
- By subcontracting much of the care and education of children and young people to a range of agencies, are we over-professionalizing parenting and minimizing the importance of the love and care that could be provided within the family or are we simply responding to the demands of modern living?
- With the increasing range of roles that modern parents fulfil alongside that of being mothers or fathers, where do they have time and space to be acknowledged for the parenting that they do carry out?
- Who parents the parents?

7 Letting go
Negotiating and facilitating independence

> **Key themes**
> - The relationship between our inner view of ourselves and how we act as parents
> - Preparation for adulthood: setting boundaries and learning to let go
> - The impact on parenting capacity of holding on to a negative family life
> - The role of parenting support in helping parents to develop independence in their children
> - Establishing examples, values and beliefs

This chapter is about developing independence, but in some important aspects it is also about setting boundaries.

The 'letting go' element relates to enabling children to make healthy choices but relinquishing some of our own control and preconceptions as parents about how our children 'ought' to behave or turn out. It is about letting go of our children in order to allow them to achieve the outcomes that are right for them and allowing them the necessary space and opportunities to develop as unique individuals, not mini-versions of ourselves.

The 'holding on' element is about the responsibilities that parents have to provide appropriate boundaries, to present an example of responsible adulthood and to shoulder the responsibility of parenting even when this is extremely difficult to do because of challenges parents face not only as parents, but also as individuals with their own needs. It is about holding on to the importance of leaving an impression, a model and script of what effective parenting and responsible living is like so that children can replicate this in their own parenting behaviour and the ways they choose to engage with the world.

Maintaining these two sides of the parenting role is probably one of the most difficult balancing acts any job can demand. In my experience, the tension involved in trying to do so is at the heart of most of the problems parents face.

Can you think of some examples of situations where parents might come into conflict with their children or each other because of differences in attitudes about what is safe and what is risky behaviour?

Dealing with inner demons

Although you may be coming to this book in order to understand and assist parenting in others, you may find yourself, as you read this chapter in particular, internalizing some of what is said here and relating it to the way that you were parented or are parenting yourself. If you do, and you find this an unsettling or uncomfortable experience, stop reading and consider seeking advice or help to work through your thoughts and feelings with someone who you trust and who will be open to listening to and supporting you. Not only will this help you to unpack and understand your own parenting behaviour but also, in turn, greater self awareness will enable you to be a better listener and facilitator of the needs of others who may be parents or who are struggling to come to terms with some of the ways in which they were brought up.

This is because competent parenting support watches, listens, thinks, remembers and understands the behaviour of the parent as well as that of the child and makes the connections between the two. It can stand back from a situation and analyse what is going on and why. It can reflect not only on what is happening in the here and now but also how inner beliefs and attitudes impact on the outward behaviour.

Developing personal constructs

We all carry around perceptions about who we are and what we are like as individuals. These views of ourselves and of our world have developed over time and reflect our external experiences and how we have internalized or made sense of these experiences as individuals. These personal constructs or understandings of not only who we are but also how we relate to and understand the world in which we live can be passed on to others.

> Can you think in your own family of any examples of characteristics that were ascribed to you or your siblings? Did you experience those individuals growing into these characteristics consciously or unconsciously: *the responsible one, the shy one, the one like his dad?*

Parents, as primary caregivers and the means by which, certainly in their earliest years, children's worlds are regulated and interpreted, play a key role in establishing children's views not only of themselves but also of their environment. The messages that parents give, either explicitly or subliminally, play a significant role in building confidence in children and reflect to a great extent the degree to which a parent feels the need to let go or hold on.

Consider, for example, the extent to which children take their cues from those around them. If a parent seems scared of spiders, children may assume that spiders are scary and learn to avoid them, even though their natural inclination might have been to find them interesting. If a parent's experience of the world has been that it is a dangerous, unforgiving and sinister place, they are likely to grow up wary and cynical – attitudes that parents can pass on explicitly or implicitly to their children.

This may have positive consequences for the child is protected from interacting with potentially dangerous influences. But there could also be negative ones if the child does not develop the ability to deal with dangers and make informed, healthy choices. An example of this happening in practice would be the increase in parents viewing the outdoors as a dangerous play space and the resulting growth for some in concern about whether children are spending too much time indoors, another example of the challenges parents face in trying to decide how best to parent.

If a parent's view of the world is more optimistic, that people are to be trusted, generally caring and altruistic and wanting only the best for us as individuals, that individual is likely to reflect this more positive outlook in their parenting and the messages they give to their children. Again, this may or may not be helpful and could result in children being overly trusting and less well equipped to make discriminating choices and decisions about interpreting the behaviour of others.

> Does it matter that a parent may be unwittingly passing on their personal view of the world to their child? Can they help to develop in their children either an optimistic or pessimistic attitude to what life will bring them? How do you think this could impact on the way that children approach challenges that they will face as they grow up?

Personal constructs and attitudes that we hold internally may be only too obvious to those around us, but are often hidden from us as individuals. They shape our behaviour often without us even realizing it. They send out messages about the world that our children – relying as they do on parents to set the conditions for their existence – both learn to live with and absorb.

It may be only when children grow up and move away from the influence of their parents that they begin to question these constructs and replace them with others that they gather from peers and the wider community. But the lessons learnt in our earliest years from our immediate carers are very powerful influences and it is sometimes years before they can be overcome.

> What's the difference between those parenting behaviours that keep a child safe and are the responsibility of parents to act upon, and those that are more about a parent's inner fears or a personal belief system that may need to be challenged by actual life experience?

Setting boundaries and managing risk

The job of safeguarding children from harm has become increasingly viewed as a legitimate area for the involvement of governments, legislation and professionals. As our views of the kind of lives that children should be leading and what childhood is for have developed we have set about creating legislative frameworks to seek to reflect this. We have laws about most aspects of children's lives: the employment of children, the amount of education to which they are entitled, how they can spend their leisure time. It could be argued that children growing up in the twenty-first century in the West, far from having more choice and freedom than their counterparts a hundred years ago, will actually encounter more regulation and a wider range of authority figures outside of the home than they ever did.

> Try to list all the regulations that surround children today, both those that are explicit like school attendance and age of consent and those that are implicit such as expectations around safety in the home or on the road. Why do you think there are so many regulations about children nowadays? How consistent are they and what do you think the impact of these could be on their development?

Some people would say there are good reasons why this has had to happen. We have become more and more aware that children face risks within the home, which is sometimes far from being a place of safety and nurture. We have many examples of parents who appear to struggle to know how to parent effectively, sometimes at even the most basic of levels.

Learning to let go with confidence

The definition of parenting support that has run through this book relates to those opportunities for parents to think, reflect and learn the necessary skills and understandings that will enable them to become more confident in achieving this balancing act between setting boundaries and enabling children to make their own choices within these. This is not about teaching a right or wrong way to parent; there is no blueprint to follow prescriptively. But when we considered parenting support in Chapter 4, it was with a perception that balancing the responsibilities of parenting was a highly challenging task at the best of times and one that becomes even more difficult if those trying to carry it out are doing so against considerable odds.

When parenting has come under the media spotlight in recent years, it is frequently because of the view that parents are setting insufficient boundaries, rather than too many. The boundaries that are set may be viewed as inappropriate for the age and stage of the child, to be inconsistently monitored, for the child either not to be rewarded or punished sufficiently or rewarded or punished too much for staying within or wandering beyond them. Parents can receive significant criticism and sanctions for letting go of their responsibilities and for not providing guidance and control for their children.

> Are there any aspects of childhood that you feel are overregulated? Do you feel that regulation enhances or inhibits the role of parents? Why do you think there has been this increase in regulation? Has there been a similar increase in any regulation about parenting support?

Teaching children to make their own decisions

Probably one of the hardest aspects of parenting in terms of achieving positive outcomes for children is deciding between the responsibility to keep a child safe and the responsibility to let a child go.

There will be general agreement at the extreme ends of this spectrum. Most individuals and cultures would expect parents (and adults in general) to protect children from the sort of physical harm that might be life threatening, although we know that even this becomes a point for debate if the child is viewed as damaged or less than 'ideal' because of cultural views about factors such as disability or gender which might lead to a foetus being aborted or even, in some cultures, a child abandoned.

Most cultures would expect parents to provide children with opportunities to unleash their natural curiosity to explore, to learn and experiment. The degree to which these learning opportunities are expected to be shaped and controlled by parents is highly individualistic and is closely tied in to environmental factors such as the amount of resources available, the perceived risks in the environment, both physical and psychological, and the view of the degree to which parents are expected to protect rather than facilitate their child's development.

As already described, how parents choose to manage these perceived risks will reveal much about that parent's view of the world. One parent's risky environment is another's learning opportunity.

While one parent may view it as their responsibility to prevent their child from experiencing a situation, another will actively encourage this to happen.

Can you think of some specific situations where parents demonstrate these differences in relation to perceived risk? Some areas to consider might be:

- attitudes towards what television programmes parents let their children watch
- the friends and peer group that parents encourage their child to associate with
- the degree to which parents monitor and control their child's leisure time.

Learning from mistakes

Parents of very small children will often look forward to the time when their children will be able to undertake many of the basic self-help behaviours of feeding, dressing, toileting and keeping clean themselves. Parents can devote many hours of the day and night to such responsibilities in relation to their children. They take time and energy. When compared to the young of other species, human infants are particularly helpless for longer in relation to these behaviours, all of which are fundamental to existence.

As children grow older we expect, in normal development, for them to be able to take more responsibility for these behaviours. The ability and willingness to do so varies between individuals but, in general, by the time children reach puberty they can undertake most of these activities independently and to a standard that, while it might not be as high as parents might have hoped, is nonetheless within a normal range. We have an expectation that parents will be letting go of these basics of care and moving to more complex and in many ways challenging aspects of parenting that involve enabling children to make their own choices about what social and moral actions to take.

This is a point when the parents of older children have been known to look back somewhat wistfully on the earlier stages of their parenting career when 'it was easier – they did as they were told.'

Observation of parent–child interactions in the earliest years would suggest that children at this stage are, in fact, also trying to make their voices heard, whether through their body language, crying or temper tantrums. They are making choices – picking up and dropping toys, selecting one activity for another, moving towards and away from different stimuli. The differences in perceptions about these behaviours lie to some extent in how we construct our view of very young children and the degree of control children have over asserting these choices when they are very young as opposed to when they get older.

There are opportunities every day, even with very young children, for parents and carers to incorporate chances for them to make choices and decisions about a whole range of aspects in their lives: their play, what they eat or drink, what they wear. They can also support even very young children to observe and learn from the consequences of their actions and the way that they can make an impact on and control even very tiny aspects of their environment.

Can you think of some examples of how those caring for children can provide opportunities for children to make choices and develop an understanding of action and consequences? How do you think this is developing a child's ability to think and act independently and take personal responsibility?

Do parents know best?

Cultural variations and attitudes towards parental authority abound. The degree to which respect for elders is ascribed to their position and age by right in a culture, rather than being viewed as something that has to be earned, not only changes over time but also is known to be influenced by one set of values coming into contact with another.

An example would be when families holding different religious beliefs begin to live in close proximity to one another or when a child of parents from a traditional background where parents are expected to take responsibility for key decisions in their child's life – how they dress, what they eat, who they marry – comes to live in a culture where children make those decisions with only passing, or in many cases seemingly no reference at all to their parents' views. Respect as a right is one thing, handing over control for decisions to adults who are themselves fallible human beings is quite another.

However, it is a challenge to address the degree to which we have embraced the rights of the individual, freedom of expression and the opening up of choice while at the same time teaching responsibility, realism and consideration for others and duty to oneself. Parenting today is about bringing up children in a world where morality is debated in a context that has fewer widely shared absolute views about rights and wrongs. Issues such as sex before marriage, abortion, divorce, rights to have a child, roles of mothers and fathers can have far more variations than in times past. This presents real challenges for parents and for children trying to navigate their way through this moral maze.

> Can you think of a topic where parents and children could have very different attitudes and values that might cause difficulties in a family? Where do you think that the responsibility lies for deciding what is right or wrong for an individual child in such circumstances? What is informing your view?

The information about the range of options for family life is also far more accessible. Images and ideas about different ways of being a family are beamed into our consciousness daily through not only television and the Internet but also what we experience first hand in our communities and families. Sometimes we have the opportunity really to get to know and understand fully the impact of these different ways of being a parent and can make informed choices and judgements. But not all the information is presented in a way that allows this to happen and we are frequently exposed to sensationalized or superficial accounts of parenting behaviours that do not allow us to get under the surface and truly understand the impact on everyone involved in how a child is raised when those involved choose particular parenting behaviours.

As a consequence, parents can find themselves ill prepared for the realities of the complications that might emerge and follow, for example, divorce or separation and may be less well equipped to anticipate, recognize and respond effectively to the feelings and behaviours those affected could experience and demonstrate.

One of the hardest things for a caring and responsible parent to do with a child who they love dearly is to stand back and watch them do something that they believe is a 'mistake'. Such behaviour flies in the face of everything that they have been trying to do in terms of protecting their child from harm. This goes right back to our discussions in Chapter 3 about parenting styles and the need to be clear about the end-point of good enough parenting.

Parents will often describe themselves as having a responsibility to protect their children from 'mistakes'. They are certainly expected to protect their children from harm. Are some 'mistakes' worth making in the short term because of the longer-term learning that they can bring? Do you think that children make mistakes that parents are there to correct or to help their child to reflect and learn from? Is life, in fact, less about avoiding mistakes and more a series of learning opportunities that parents are there to facilitate?

In the normal course of events parents will, one day, not be there physically to protect their children. They will not be able to tell their child how to behave or to control the choices they make.

If a part of growing up is learning to become our own parent, is it not important that we practise making our own decisions and taking responsibility for and ownership of those? If children do not get practice at doing this when they are young, of internalizing their understanding of right and wrong, action and consequences, how equipped are they going to be to do so when they are older?

Some cultures and religious communities are much clearer about the responsibilities parents have to direct their children and tougher on parents who do not set an 'appropriate' example. However, even in such cultures there is an expectation that the child will grow to understand the reasons for this approach and make this the foundation in turn for their own future choices about how they parent their own children.

Unless parents learn to move away from always directing a child's life, and take responsibility for allowing at least some space for the child to 'take the wheel' sometimes, they will be meeting only one side of their responsibilities in relation to protecting their children from harm and failing to develop in their children the ability to make their own decisions.

Is it ever too young to give children choices or is this parents' abdicating their responsibility to provide guidance and direction?

Knowing when to let go

Making a judgement about when to stand back from a child and when to intervene is probably one of the toughest calls for any parent. It is reasonably straightforward where physical safety is concerned, for example protecting a child from being run over, burnt, drowned or injured. It is far more difficult where the risk is in the future or only a statistical possibility. Parents might think:

- Miss out on this education and you might not get employment.
- Mix with this peer group and you might get into trouble.
- Wear those clothes and you could attract negative attention.
- Stay out late and you might get attacked.

In such situations parents and children weigh relative risks and may well come to very different conclusions based on their experience of the world to date. Children might think:

- Get an education and I still might not get a job.
- Lose these friends and I might not get any more.
- Wear different clothes and people won't accept me.
- Come home early and I'll miss out on the fun.

Equally, these lists might be switched around, with parents thinking the second set of risks might apply to their offspring and children the first. In turn, this may lead to particular responses in either camp, with parents and children turning for the type of support that they feel will reinforce whichever of the outcomes they perceive to be most appropriate.

Most parents become aware as their parenting journey develops that there are gaps between their view of the world and that of their children. In Chapter 6 we looked at the significance of the *intention* of the parent, how they choose to interpret the circumstances of a situation, for the type of support that they feel it demands. The differences in the behaviour of the parent arising from how they attach meaning to the situation are a function of a complex interplay between the parents themselves, the characteristics and needs they see in their children (which will almost certainly contribute to them choosing to respond differently to different children because they view them individually as having different levels of vulnerability) and the particular set of circumstances that they perceive in the environment at any one time.

Siblings brought up by the same parents often describe inconsistencies between what those parents allowed one child in the family to do rather than another. From the children's perspective this can seem very unfair and irrational: why does one child get away with behaviour that another does not?

Why might parents treat their children differently and how might some of the decisions they make be affected by the context and the meaning they attach to their responsibilities to respond as parents to the personalities and needs of the individual children?

How parents and children manage to negotiate their way through these differences is the basis for the relationship that they have throughout their time together and even when they are apart. It is often a source of tension and disagreements and may bring parents face to face with the degree to which their hopes and dreams for their children fit with the ones that those children develop for themselves.

Does a good parent sometimes stand back and allow a child to do something that the parent believes will make that child unhappy? What can parents do to support the quality of the ongoing relationship between them and their child at such times? What happens if they continue to show compassion for their child even though they are doing something they feel as parents is a mistake or alternatively they choose to put a distance between them because of the decisions they have made?

Finding our own paths

'In child' factors, physical and mental capabilities, personalities and traits have a significant impact on how children develop. The genetic similarities between parents and children mean that they often share these traits and characteristics and parents may either want to develop these or do everything they can to prevent their child 'making the same mistakes' they perceive themselves or their partners as having made.

Sometimes it is extremely difficult for parents to recognize that what they actually want for their child will not be realized because that, quite simply, is not who their child is or is capable of or was meant to be.

Children are not colouring books. None of us is an exact replica of our parents or a perfect rendition of what they were expecting and we will not make the same decisions or necessarily adopt the same view of the world. There is a balance in our lives between predestination – some outcomes are statistically more likely from particular starting points – and free will: every one of our choices and decisions along the way helps to shape the next steps. Children will want and quite rightly need to map out their own paths in life and to leave their own footprints in history.

> Have you ever experienced or read about this sense of failing to 'live up to' the expectations of a parent? Do you agree that it can have a powerful impact on the parent-child dynamic as they adjust and learn to accept each other for who they are? How important is it that they each do?

That is not to say, however, that parents do not matter or do not have a place in establishing these paths. Parents have other experiences on which to draw and, because they share characteristics with their children, will have some of the same tendencies and traits. Children are children and, in our society, we demonstrate through our social, educational, legal and political structures and systems that we expect children to have less responsibility, to be less accountable and to enjoy greater protection than adults. We expect adults, parents in particular, to moderate and guide the behaviour of children in general. While we may expect social, economic and political policy to create the conditions within which children will be enabled to grow and develop, we expect parents to apply this to the specific needs of their individual children.

How might the genetic predisposition, characteristics or physicality of a child influence the dreams a parent might have for what their child might become? How can this be a problem:

- for the parent?
- for the child?
- for society?

The role of parenting support in enabling parents to make effective judgements about letting go

Parenting support is activity that enables parents to develop the skills and insights to carry out the parenting role. We have explored at length in Chapters 4, 5 and 6 the importance of the intention of parenting support and of having access to the kind that provides information about what to do in different parenting situations, the ability to step back from a particular set of circumstances and reflect on why it is happening and the relevance of nurturing parents as people.

Parenting is about an intensely personal relationship between two individuals and the judgements that each makes about how to conduct those interactions. Other people can offer advice and guidance, and frequently do, but ultimately this is a relationship which begins with a power imbalance that must, over time, adapt and respond to changes in the needs of parent and child if it is to result in mutual respect and independence, acceptance and love.

Having children is the most natural thing in the world; being good at parenting is probably the hardest. Getting the balance between holding tight and letting go is very tough, but parents who are holding tight to a child may live to see them struggle to be free to be the person they choose to be, not the person their parent might think they should be.

It could be argued that making these judgements, knowing when to hold on or let go, is essentially what effective parenting is about. While every parent ultimately has to make these decisions for themselves, having people to turn to, experiences to draw on and places to go for guidance, advice and reassurance has been shown time and again to be so important for parents, whatever their age, stage, background or experience (Golding 2000; Kazdin 1997).

Although we can provide parenting support in a variety of forms, ultimately the quality of the parenting that children experience reflects some inner sense of what their parent believes, at a particular point in time, to be the right thing to do. We might try to separate out the degree to which that is a product of instinct, social norms, personal experience but, ultimately, it results in behaviours that, in turn, will shape the next generation.

> What characteristics do you feel would be helpful for people to have in order to facilitate a parent's personal reflection on how their behaviour might be holding a child back rather than enabling them to become independent? Where might parents be able to access such support in their communities and those providing it be able to develop the skills to do so?

Relationships that enable rather than undermine parenting capacity

There are so many elements of family life that impact on the capacity to parent effectively and many of these relate to the relationship between the parents themselves. I have known some parenting support actually to lead to parents leaving each other because they come to recognize that the relationship between them is so destructive for the adults within it that it is, in turn, damaging the outcomes for the children.

Ending, rather than remaining with a parenting relationship 'for the sake of the children', might be necessary to release the necessary emotional energy to parent effectively or to put the parent and their children into a place of safety so that the parent that ultimately has the care and responsibility for the children can fulfil their parenting role. We should not underestimate support parents need not only as parents but also as individuals with their own needs to achieve this separation in ways that leave all involved feeling secure and safe.

How do you feel about the idea that parenting support could lead to parents finding the strength to separate 'for the sake of the children', rather than remaining together? What are the implications for the wider family support that needs to be available if this were to happen and how do those parents continue to negotiate their parenting behaviour for the sake of the children, even though they may no longer live together?

The parenting journey is hard enough without carrying or holding on to difficult and destructive burdens that are weighing us down. Sometimes it is obvious what these burdens are, or obvious to others but not necessarily to ourselves. They may be relationships that are unhelpful or demanding. It could be responsibilities that we are choosing to take on or we are being expected to undertake arising from our roles or employment. Very often it will be inner beliefs based on our view of ourselves and what we feel we 'ought' to be that will weigh us down.

Sometimes there are actions parents can take to remove themselves from a really damaging or dangerous relationship or set of responsibilities which are so threatening to the physical and emotional well-being of the family members that there is no choice but to bring the situation to an end. In many ways, although incredibly upsetting, when a situation has reached such a threshold, at least the decision that leaving the relationship or setting aside the responsibility is the right course of action is more clear cut, albeit often very hard to carry through. We often recognize that making significant changes might create conflict in terms of access to the children or other family members and may require considerable investment on the part of all involved to be able to handle the situation without doing even further damage.

More often, what many families will encounter are less clear cut, critical incidents that signal a clear tipping-point has been reached and suggesting that the relationship has to end or the context in which the family is trying to exist needs to change. Far more likely is that there will be difficulties in relationships or the family lifestyle that have an impact on parenting capacity but that are not so significant that individuals are very obviously in danger. Sometimes, if we are very fortunate, this means finding a way to draw attention to the problems we face and getting support to deal with them sooner rather than later. This is not easy in a society that is increasingly complex, arguably not paying coordinated and focused attention on family life until things are very serious and losing some of the networks of support through religious organizations, neighbourhoods or family networks that might have drawn attention to and offered the kind of practical help that could have kept the situation manageable for those involved.

> How accessible is parenting support in communities before problems become really serious? Can informal networks, help lines, information in the media, self-help groups and drop-ins in the community bridge the gap between universal and specialist services for parents?

Being honest

Parents do not, by and large, set out to have problems with their children. Their child is born and a journey begins, but everything about that journey brings those involved face to face with the limitations in themselves, those around them and the society in which they exist. Being alone, either physically or emotionally as a parent, just makes the workload involved in the journey heavier, but even when parenting in a partnership it is possible to feel emotionally alone.

'Letting go' involves parents relinquishing some of those images not only of a perfect child, but also of themselves as perfect parents. Parents who take part in parenting programmes frequently comment on the relief they feel when they recognize that they are not alone in facing problems with their children; it goes with the territory and does not mean that they cannot make a difference or should give up.

This element of the parenting journey involves really being honest and facing up to individual limitations:

- 'Maybe if I was more capable I could deal with this situation, but right now, I don't have the skills or abilities to do so.'
- 'If I had known then what I know now I'd have taken a completely different approach.'
- 'Once I started on that path there just didn't seem any way back.'

This is not an excuse to do nothing, however. Recognizing limitations is a first step towards owning a problem. Owning a problem is a first step towards taking responsibility. Taking responsibility is a first step towards change. That change might take parents and children on a whole new route, but still enables parents to fulfil their responsibilities to give children the best parenting experience they possibly can.

Questions to consider

- This chapter has argued that parents need to learn to balance taking responsibility for their children's safety with helping them to develop independence. Do all parents find it hard to let go of their children, or are some failing to hold on appropriately?
- How hard is it for parents to seek help for their parenting relationships, or aspects of their family life that impact on their parenting? Where do the barriers come from: the availability of support, the fear of being judged, the lack of awareness of the impact of these issues on the outcomes for their children or an inability on the part of the parents to face up to the realities of a situation?
- Counselling services often provide support for adults to help them to manage problems within their relationships with their partners or to deal with issues they face such as domestic violence, addiction, depression and mental health. How important is it for these services to recognize these adults as parents and to take on board the impact of these issues on the children of these individuals?

8 Leaving a legacy

Key themes
- The perspective that no parent would feel alone if parenting support were viewed as an entitlement for all
- The debate about the parenting and family support that already exists within communities
- The potential role of government in enabling parenting support to be part of mainstream provision
- The impact of parenting support on outcomes for children

The place of parenting support as an essential part of service delivery

Throughout this book I have continually returned to the theme of whether parents matter to outcomes for children. I hope that I have emphasized sufficiently that there is considerable evidence that they do. Having activities that enable parents to develop skills and confidence in their role could exist alongside wider family support in all of our communities and for every different type of parenting situation. Parents are still the people most likely to be continuously involved with their children and supporting them to carry out and enjoy their role makes good social, psychological and economic sense. From my perspective, it also just feels like the right thing to do.

We give a significant amount of energy and resources to the other aspects of our development: our education, our health, where we live, our friendships, how we spend our leisure time. But if parents do matter, making the space to understand the part that our parents have played in who we are and their contribution to the puzzle that is each and every one of us is also important. To achieve positive outcomes for children we need confident parents and positive memories of parenting from which in turn to draw the strength to be confident parents of confident children ourselves.

From this perspective, parents matter in terms of the legacy that they leave to the next generation. It is children who will take the world forward long after their parents are little more than a distant memory.

Some of the outcomes that arguably arise from effective parenting: the ability to form loving and accepting relationships, respect for difference and enjoyment of each other as people is a basis for every subsequent human relationship we encounter as we grow up.

> To what extent do you think that parents can help to equip their children with these abilities to form successful relationships with others? How do they do this and apart from their parents where else do children learn their values and attitudes about others?

Although as a society we expect parents to take their responsibilities seriously, we know that parenting can be a rollercoaster ride, because people are imperfect and parenting has highs and lows. Relationships between parents and children can be not only some of the most wonderful, but also some of the most challenging and complex of our lives. Parenting is a multifaceted role. We really should not expect anyone to be good at every element of it naturally.

> Do you feel as a society that we value parents and support them as much for what they are doing well as for where they may be struggling? Should we be doing more to recognize and celebrate what parents do? What difference do you think it would make if parents and children spent more time celebrating and enjoying family life?

When the relationships are working well, we see parents and children enjoying each other's company in the here and now. The degree to which parents and children love and respect each other may be hard to measure, but it could be argued that in developing social and family policy it warrants attention as something that we need to debate and to ensure is being fostered.

> What messages do you think it gives children when they are treated as individuals, shown special attention, guided and challenged and made

to feel secure and loved by their parents? What kinds of things that happen in families, schools and communities enable this to happen and what undermines this? How can we use parenting support to enable individuals to show respect for themselves and to demonstrate respect for others?

Being clear about where we are heading

My central theme has been that parents matter because the way that they carry out and are enabled to carry out their role has a huge impact on outcomes for children. If we agree that this is the case and if we are serious about achieving these outcomes *for all children*, it is hard to see how we have any choice but to be persistent and tenacious in our pursuit of parenting support as an entitlement *for all parents*.

As ever, language is crucial. It is easy to confuse 'outcomes' (the impact of what we do) with 'outputs' (what we do). No wonder parents can feel pressurized when family members, teachers, social workers, the media, the police, to name a few, can all appear to have differing views about what parents should do. In Chapter 1, I suggested that, as a society, we appear unclear about what constitutes 'good' parenting and that we perhaps need a wider debate about what we would see and hear 'good' parents – fathers and mothers – doing to warrant that description.

What is the 'end-point' of effective parenting? Is it the job the child eventually holds down, their qualifications, the car they drive, where they live, their values and beliefs, or their awareness of how their behaviour impacts on others? How might being clear about these end-points help to inform the way that we choose to parent our children, the time we spend with them and the choices that we make in relation to their care and education?

If we accept that it is our children who are the greatest resource that we have for the future, and if failing to make the most of any resource is wasteful and problematic, then making a mess of our children as a resource is downright wrong. I would argue that it behoves all of us, not just those who are parents, to do whatever we can to create the conditions in which our children will thrive now and in the future.

The way ahead: politically and personally

What is different and what is the same about parenting now as opposed to in previous generations? Broadly, there are more choices now about how to parent, more models, fewer moral absolutes around issues such as abortion, sex before marriage, same sex partnerships, divorce, fathering, mothering. The world is filled with more socially accepted options and different models to choose from and this is coupled with greater affluence (actual or aspirational), freedom of expression, availability of travel and wider experiences.

We may have more choice, but we still need to be able to balance rights with responsibilities, freedom with respect and our interconnectedness and ever growing awareness of how what happens in one part of a global economy has an impact on another.

We may be more connected at some levels, but we also need to feel centred, that we 'matter' as individuals. We may achieve this feeling through different routes, through having a personal relationship we can rely on, feeling special and unique rather than just a number or a client, through having a home, financial security, a job or a role, a routine, personal goals and a realistic means to attain them.

> To what extent do parents play a role in establishing these means to establish these outcomes? How might parents support or undermine our
>
> - need to be treated as an individual
> - need to be listened to
> - need to feel special, precious, valuable
> - need to feel safe and secure.

The outcomes that individuals and a society as a whole choose to promote reflect what they value. Where we choose to invest our greatest resources is an indication of our beliefs about what is important: morally, ethically, politically and socially. Does the evidence suggest to you that children and childhood are valued in their own right?

Traditionally western governments have been reluctant to step into family life in ways that could suggest they are telling parents how to bring up their children unless there is a real risk of harm. How does this fit with the role of government to enable the best outcomes for children if parenting is such a significant factor for these outcomes? Parents may need access to support that respects their differences and acknowledges that one size does not fit all. This should be reflected in the way that they are able to access support in their communities not only from friends and family but also from professionals.

Chapter 4 described the way in which parenting support from professionals became more generally available in communities as something offered as part of the role of many different practitioners but that gradually began to adopt significance in its own right. The introduction of parenting support strategies, senior parenting practitioners, parenting commissioners and evidence-based parenting programmes into the mainstream of service delivery in every local authority in the UK in the early part of the twenty-first century had the potential to be highly significant for the world of parenting support in the future. The moves towards developing a specific training pathway for parenting practitioners initially through the National Academy for Parenting Practitioners and then with the input of the Children's Workforce and Development Council was another recognition of the emerging understanding of the sorts of knowledge, skills and attitudes that effective parenting practitioners needed. Work on linking aspects of parenting support to national indicators, service targets and outcomes for children begun towards the end of 2009 potentially laid a foundation for future debate about this whole area and this was a period when we saw a focus beginning to emerge on making these links explicit.

All parents need support, but some parenting situations mean that people require more support than others for the short or longer term. It is fair to assume (and there is plenty of research evidence to support the assumption) that the earlier and more appropriate the support and the better the fit between the assessed needs and the intervention, the more likely it is to achieve a positive outcome. Equal rights however do not mean equal needs, which is why support has to be differentiated to be effective.

> Thomas Jefferson once said that all men are created equal . . . There is a tendency . . . for certain people to use this phrase out of context, to satisfy all conditions . . . We know that all men are not created equal in the sense some people would

have us believe – some people are smarter than others, some people have more opportunity because they are born with it, some men make more money than others, some ladies make better cakes than others – some people are born gifted beyond the normal scope of most men.

(Lee 2004: 223)

How much importance do you feel we attach in our society to providing early universal support for parents that is tailored to meet their needs in the here and now and promoting the conditions whereby we enable parents and children to develop positive relationships with each other? What form might a differentiated approach to providing parenting support as a universal, targeted or specialist service look like in practice? What advantages and disadvantages could there be to having parenting support available as an entitlement for all rather than something that only parents perceived to be having significant problems could access?

In conclusion, I would like to reflect on the impact of parents and parenting behaviour on each of the Every Child Matters outcomes for children. I do so because I think parenting is about leaving a legacy. These outcomes do matter and there is a real sense in which parents hold a key to them all.

Are we drawing on what we know works in terms of supporting effective parenting and using this information and understanding to develop the kinds of persistent, challenging and dynamic and supportive services and relationships to make sure this happens? How much progress do you feel has been made in bringing parenting and family support services closer together and creating flexible, local and responsive service provision that is both tiered and integrated across adults' and children's services?

Leaving a legacy: being healthy

> To what extent are we acknowledging the work that parents need to carry out to ensure their child is healthy? How are we challenging and supporting parents to be role models that children would wish to emulate? What do children see when they look at their parents? Do they see people that, within their personal limitations are healthy, both physically and emotionally? To what extent are parents enabled to take responsibility for modelling respect for their own bodies and being recognized for doing so?

We know that children are far more likely to smoke, abuse alcohol and take drugs if those who bring them up do so as well. We know that children who witness domestic violence are far more likely to be victims or perpetrators of violence themselves. There is very strong evidence that parents who have a poor diet produce overweight or poorly nourished children – even when they have the resources to be different (Burniat et al. 2006; Poskitt and Edmunds 2008). There is a degree of personal responsibility in this, but also some collective duties. How are we as a society persistently and constructively addressing this?

Leaving a legacy: staying safe

> Attitudes to risk can have a huge impact on the way that children develop. In families where adults take significant risks with relationships and finances, children learn from first-hand experience the impact of this on their personal security. If everyone around them is taking similar risks, one could argue that this situation just becomes the norm and no one seems too bothered or disturbed. It's just how it is. To what extent do you feel this is recognized or acknowledged in families and communities?

There is strong evidence that allowing children to experience some risk enables them to learn about making safe choices (Tovey 2007). Wrapping children in cotton wool so that they never learn about dangers and how to deal with challenge is not good for their ability to develop independence. However, reflecting on the longer-term impact of taking risks, particularly with relationships, is quite sobering. We are probably not going to return to the situation where people 'stayed together for the sake of the children' but we should certainly consider how in separating from relationships we enable parents to take on board not only their own needs but also the rights of the children involved and to address their need to feel safe and secure before, during and after such separations.

Leaving a legacy: enjoying and achieving

Do schools and Sure Start Children's Centres have a key role to play in terms of enabling parents to support this outcome for children as institutions that are identifiable in communities that are part of the whole village that it takes to bring up a child? How do we enable them to feel they are part of a team with collective responsibility for those outcomes, but specific roles and responsibilities within that? How might this form part of the extended schools agenda?

Partnerships between home and school, parents and teachers, in order to develop children's learning, have a reasonable tradition (Wolfendale 2002). With the advent of extended schools and Sure Start Children's Centres came a growing focus on each of these as hubs in communities where information about wider family and parenting support services could be accessed. There had long been a tradition of using schools as a universal service from which to build relationships with parents in communities and the capacity for this work was enhanced with the development of a new role of parent support adviser (Training and Development Agency for Schools 2009). These individuals, generally based in one or between a number of different schools serving an identified school community, were used to communicate messages and understandings between home and school. These roles became recognized as increasingly significant in the mix but it was sometimes difficult to articulate how that activity made a specific difference to outcomes for children. Not every school used them all the time to provide parenting support; sometimes they were more of a classroom assistant or filled a gap between school and children's social care taking on a heavy casework role with specific families requiring a high level of supervision.

> Our schools are still judged primarily for the learning that children achieve and this in turn and inevitably impacts on how teachers view parents and their role with their children. While we have developed policy after policy that focuses on schools as hubs of community activity, do we still emphasize the role of schools as centres of academic learning rather than emotional well-being? Would this be less problematic if teachers had more space and support themselves to more readily be part of the wider children's services team?

I have heard teachers, like other practitioners, at times begrudging doing paperwork to evidence their outputs. We do need to show what we are doing, but to what extent should the evidence of impact be the behaviour and attitudes of the children, not the neatly written-up lesson plans or self-assessment documents? If the record keeping, information sharing and data collecting enable us to be more effective and to better understand why we are doing something, it has a benefit. If it is simply repeating data that is held elsewhere or an end in itself, we should consider why we are doing it. If it is a management tool that is used to check up on whether people are carrying out activity, that could be done through observation and discussion. If all this record keeping is worth doing, it should be mutually understood to be in relation to how it is used: to enable us to reflect on and change practice in order to be more effective.

Leaving a legacy: making a positive contribution

> To what extent are we valuing parents for modelling a commitment to the world in which they live? Do they show appreciation and reinforce behaviour that is helpful and likely to improve the community and make it more cohesive or do they promote hatred and anarchy? Are

> parents celebrated when they support members of the community that are less able, looking out for one another within the home, caring for the environment?

The attitudes and values that children have about themselves and others are first developed at home. Time and again parents who come into parenting programmes or other types of parenting support say that where it worked well, they were both supported to recognize the contribution they were making and challenged to develop this still further. The facilitators were skilled enough to enable parents to recognize not only what they had to offer but also how they could make an even greater contribution by listening and tuning in to themselves and their children.

Effective parenting support, like effective parenting, leads to change. In order to change, we have to recognize that what is happening now is not working, is not good enough, could and should be better and that we have the power, the responsibility and the resources to make that change. This requires leadership. It requires a space to be created where it is safe to acknowledge and to be honest about the situation, to recognize that it is not acceptable to be in this position and to feel able to progress from it. Without such leadership and space, we will often encounter defensiveness, resistance and even aggression.

> The purpose of parenting support is to empower parents to identify their own strengths as parents, as well as their issues for learning and development.
>
> (DCSF 2009c: 4)

> To what extent is a role of communities, whether these are families, schools or religious institutions, to create a culture where it is acceptable to take responsibilities for actions – even if doing so brings an individual to a place where they feel bad for a while – but to do this alongside a clearly defined set of people with roles that show genuine acceptance of us, and enable us to move forward? How might doing this for parents improve their ability and their capacity to improve outcomes for their children?

Leaving a legacy: achieving economic well-being

One of my earlier questions was if we placed too much emphasis on children as a resource, would we tend to focus primarily on what they produce – their outputs, rather than the difference they make – their outcome and whether this risked reducing human beings to commodities with their value being measured more in terms of what they produce or consume than the difference they might make morally or spiritually.

This is about parents not just being viewed as having done a good job because they have children who are in paid employment or materially well off. This is also about parents encouraging their children to develop their gifts and talents and to be caring and supportive as citizens. It relates to parents teaching their children to look out for others, not only to aspire but also to recognize the value of being happy and contented because of what a person has now that meets their actual needs, rather than reinforcing materialism and greed.

Leaving a legacy: being emotionally intelligent

Throughout this book I have made reference to the importance of parents celebrating and living in the moment, building relationships between themselves and their children that show they love each other as people, even if they do not always like some of the actions that they might take. Parents can help children to become people who take responsibility for their own decisions, to be able to articulate why they are doing what they are doing, to make informed choices that not only make them feel good in the short term but also recognize their impact on longer-term consequences. As the world becomes ever more interconnected, it becomes increasingly significant for all of us for this to happen.

Parenting support as a form of safeguarding: turning the curve

If we had a leaking roof we would know about it. We could measure the amount of water dripping through by catching it in a bucket. We might see a damp patch on the ceiling and monitor how far it spreads over time. There would be things we could do. If we had a ladder we could get up on the roof and mend any broken tiles. If things got really serious, we could contact our insurance companies and see if they would fund a new roof. Or we could just ignore the problem, cross our fingers and hope that it would go away.

We all know the risks involved in leaving a small problem and hoping that it will somehow right itself. Our experience teaches us that a leaking roof that is not dealt with early stores up a potentially much more expensive and potentially catastrophic problem for the future.

When Friedman (2005) talks about 'turning the curve', he uses the leaking roof analogy and applies it to a whole range of social issues which if not addressed early and fixed will escalate. He describes what will happen if we do not change the progress of a line on a graph that is heading in a particular direction and enable it to 'turn the curve' towards the outcome we actually want to see. That outcome might be a roof that is no longer leaking or a whole range of social behaviours: teenage pregnancy rates going down rather than increasing, attainment improving rather than standing still, attendance at school getting better rather than worse. What he focuses on is identifying the range of activities that could be undertaken that have a reasonable chance of changing the direction of travel on the graph and then focusing resources: time, energy, funding on those that can demonstrate they make the biggest impact. Generally speaking, unlike with fixing a roof, social issues are caused by a complex range of factors that require people to pool ideas and resources and work together for the same outcomes.

This presupposes first that we know what those outcomes are, and it could be argued that the Every Child Matters agenda took us some way closer to being at a point where we had a clear articulation of those outcomes. The next stage involves agreeing how we get there and what cross-cutting themes such as information sharing, better engagement and participation, developing the knowledge, skills and value base of staff, better assessment of need and fit of earlier intervention to need, that run through them all might enable this to happen.

For me, it will be crucial that we consider and measure the impact of government policies, community engagement and family behaviour on parenting as part of achieving those outcomes. Does focusing in an intelligent, reflective and joined-up way on developing effective parenting enable us to turn the curve around each or any of the ECM outcomes?

The Children's Plan set out ambitions to make England the best place in the world for children and young people to grow up. Parents play the most important role in making this happen ... Parenting support is ultimately aimed at helping parents to improve outcomes for their children's behaviour, achievements, well-being and prospects for the future as well as providing measurable benefits for parents themselves. Support for parents takes many forms and has many different aims. In order to determine whether these aims have been met parenting commissioners have asked:

- What difference can we really make?
- How effective is the support we are offering?
- Is it really making a difference to the lives of children and their parents?
- Is what we are doing adding value and making best use of all available resources?
- What real changes have resulted from this investment of time, effort, training and money?

The parenting outcomes framework was commissioned ... to focus ... attention on the impact and outcomes of support activity ... to gather, measure and analyse the evidence in a robust and consistent way ... support models of commissioning, decommissioning and performance management of parenting strategies and influence future funding decisions.

(DCSF 2009c: 2)

Since the first parenting programmes emerged in the latter part of the twentieth century, there had gradually emerged a growing policy focus on addressing the responsibilities of parents to be able to provide some of the elements that we know enable children to develop into strong, emotionally intelligent citizens. Linking the review of parenting strategies to these ECM outcomes would be a key step in building this understanding and establishing the relevance of parenting support to those outcomes.

The workforce reform agenda: if only we had more people like . . .

History teaches us that for change to happen, we need leaders with vision, determination, energy and commitment who can unite people around a common goal. It is likely that for change to take place in the way that services for children and families will be delivered throughout the rest of the twenty-first century and on into the future, we will need this style of leadership at all levels: on the frontline, in the community, at head of service and at the strategic levels. We know that all those involved in any change process need knowledge, skills and values in order to be able to rise to the challenges they will face. Some of this will come from their professional training, some from other staff development opportunities, some from professional or personal experience. Some of these attributes could be said to be 'just the way they are'. Together they contribute to establishing the sorts of people that can make change happen.

What follows is my analysis of the five steps that are followed when such people do provide effective parenting support.

Step 1 Signpost: letting people know what's available

We have a whole range of ways of doing this, for example, one-stop shops, families' information services, advertising, word of mouth. All of these are useful in raising awareness but turning that awareness into action is still a significant step.

Step 2 Scaffold: understanding the steps between where a person is now and where they need to get to, breaking this down into smaller steps and establishing an individual plan for moving from one to the other

This requires attention and time and knowledge of the individuals concerned, including their context, much like my earlier 'bath books' illustration. What seems like a simple step to one person can seem huge to another. This is so often where parenting support practitioners in the community have such a key role because they are visible and could build those bridges. The really skilled ones can enable both professionals to see how they came across to parents and parents to see how they come across to professionals.

Step 3 Support: getting alongside, listening, relationship building, understanding

There is significant challenge in enabling people to move from wanting just to learn what would 'cure' their problem into an engagement with a potential change in their own behaviour. Often people that come into public service – particularly to work with children and families – will say that they came into it 'to make a difference'. If they are to do this in a way that enables and empowers people to be more independent, they will need to help people to change, to become less reliant on their external support, more resourceful and stronger in themselves. Often frustration arises from the feeling that these individuals do not have the necessary space or time to get to know families well enough to do this effectively or at a point when a situation could be improved substantially before it becomes a crisis.

If we do not establish a sense of shared responsibility for the outcomes for the children in the community, we potentially leave those dealing with their greatest crises, such as social workers, with the burden of this. We should not be surprised when they become worn down or we have difficulty in recruiting to the profession.

Step 4 Safeguard: providing challenge and making judgements about thresholds for interventions

It is enjoyable for most of us to offer support, reassurance and praise. It can be extremely uncomfortable by comparison to challenge and it requires significant skill and leadership to do so in ways that lead to the change needed.

It is difficult to talk about safeguarding and challenge without talking about power. Where individuals have control or status or authority it becomes extremely difficult for those perceived as having less power and authority to challenge. This goes for the following examples:

- Parents challenging a head teacher's perception that the school is 'doing everything' it can to tackle bullying.
- A parent support adviser challenging a head teacher that the school is 'doing everything' to engage parents effectively in their child's learning.
- A parenting support practitioner challenging a parent to prioritize meeting their child's needs and to set boundaries for their children and take up their responsibilities to monitor them.
- A social worker making judgements about how fit a parent is to maintain responsibility for their child.
- A parenting commissioner challenging service managers to create space in key staff's time to deliver parenting programmes and build parenting support into the day jobs of identified staff and to recognize their need to build the skills to deliver these effectively.
- A director of children's services challenging colleagues from other agencies to focus on outcomes for children when working with adult clients who are also parents.

Step 5 Celebrate: building on the positives and moving forward on these

Often this is quite hard to do because on a day-to-day basis we see such small changes and can find ourselves focusing on how far there is still to go. There may be a sense in which the goalposts are perceived to be constantly moving as a government increasingly views itself as having a role in enabling the conditions for families to bring up their children effectively, while at the same time reiterating that it is right for parents to raise their own children. This is a difficult message to manage because we also do expect authorities to step in when parents appear not to be controlling their children or providing for their children appropriately.

Creating the culture

When developing the Parenting Strategy in the local authority where I was working at the time, we consulted with over 700 people to try to get a picture of what, from their perspectives, would make the difference in terms of outcomes for children in relation to parenting support. Although people talked about resources and time, over and over again they also talked about the characteristics of the people involved – both parents and practitioners – their knowledge, skills, values and beliefs. Very often they described anecdotally particular individuals, the 'real gems' who, they felt, in an ideal world, they would just replicate. Essentially they are individuals who are able to put into practice the five engagement steps I have outlined above. These people have a variety of different roles and job titles, but they are all described as generally demonstrating some or all of the following characteristics:

- Never gives up, is persistent and dogged
- Knows what's available in the area from a wide range of agencies
- Returns your calls, does what they say they will
- Shows respect for self, families and other practitioners
- Does not judge, but has high standards
- Shows a sense of humour
- Knows own limitations, but is willing to think outside the box
- Recognizes and will respond to thresholds for child protection issues
- Has a can do approach, but is realistic and honest about the need for small steps
- Tailors input to need in a creative and original way
- Challenges services to get and stay involved
- Is an excellent communicator in lots of circumstances
- Has a sound understanding of normal child development
- Maintains credibility when giving parenting advice
- Has an excellent awareness of impact of family circumstances on needs.

It is worth considering which of these characteristics could be described as knowledge, which are skills and which are values and beliefs. Some may be more than one of these. If we think these characteristics are important and we recognize that they are indeed present in people who really make a difference and act as change agents, how do we develop them in everyone? Can some be developed through initial professional qualifications, staff training, or through opportunities to mentor or to shadow others? Are some of these 'just the way we are'?

Who is the client?

I recently had a conversation with a service manager, who was berating the way that services for children are being expected to change and take on board those activities that are proving to be most effective in terms of outcomes and to stop doing those that did not. He said: 'People are feeling tired with all these new ways of working and the growing expectation to share more information and get to know a wider network of practitioners. We're just not looking after the staff.'

Here are some questions that I think we need to ask when we hear this type of comment:

- Who is the service for, the staff or the children and their families?
- Is there evidence that the service is delivering all the outcomes for its client group of children and families that are needed as it is currently configured?
- If, for example, there are outcomes that are heading in the wrong direction, is there any evidence that changing the way the service is delivered would help to turn the curve?
- Whose responsibility is it to find that out?
- What do vulnerable children and families say about the extent to which the service is meeting their needs?
- Who has more to lose from the service not changing – the staff or the families they are there to serve?
- How are we supporting and developing the leaders in our communities and services to make these changes happen?

Of course change is hard. But is it fair that we go time and again to the people that show the tenacity, determination and empathy that make a real difference to outcomes for children and families? Is it not important to provide the persistent leadership, challenge and support that establish the sorts of integrated, responsible and respectful service delivery that is crucial for people to change?

The parenting adventure

I could never have known how much I could love my children or how extraordinarily privileged I feel to have been a part of their lives.

Nothing at all prepared me for the peace and contentment it has given me to know them, nor the trouble, worry and anxiety that the relationship has sometimes caused.

Parents cannot respond effectively to these situations alone. The evidence suggests that they benefit from support through having challenging but safe, thoughtful and reflective conversations with family and friends to explore their feelings about the relationships they have with their children and to plan what they are going to do and how they are going to behave towards them. They also need social, economic and political policies that clearly underline the significance that we place on their role and of enabling them to fulfil it.

This has less to do with focusing on outcomes for the future and more with debating our values and beliefs about the kind of society we want to live in right now.

There will be a parent-shaped piece of the puzzle missing in each of us if we are not enabled one day to become our own parent. It has been said that it takes a whole village to raise a child. I believe it takes a whole intergenerational community to raise and continuously support and challenge us as parents.

If we are serious about achieving better outcomes for children, we need to demonstrate, through leadership at all levels and support and engagement embedded in each of those communities, that we truly believe every parent matters.

Questions to consider

- What kind of society do we want to live in? One where:
  - Parents are viewed as the problem and we have more punishments for parents and a blame culture?
  - Parents are viewed as part of the solution and we have more parenting support which isviewed as 'normal' and is embedded in local communities?
  - Better outcomes for children where we have more informed, balanced and joined-up policies for children

and families and effective, integrated, early intervention and service delivery involving parenting and family support tailored to need?

- If you could identify just three ways to 'turn the curve' in relation to developing parenting support that would lead to better outcomes for children, what would they be?
- What have you done already and what are you going to do next to make those changes happen?

Useful websites

Cabinet Office
www.cabinetoffice.gov.uk

Chartered Institute of Personnel and Development
www.cipd.co.uk

Children's Society
www.childrenssociety.org.uk

Coalition on Men and Boys
www.comab.org.uk

Department for Children, Schools and Families
www.dcsf.gov.uk

Every Child Matters
www.dcsf.gov.uk/everychildmatters

Every Parent Matters
www.dcsf.gov.uk/everychildmatters/resources-and-practice/IG00219

Family Learning
www.familylearning.org.uk

Fatherhood Institute
www.fatherhoodinstitute.org

National Academy for Parenting Practitioners
www.parentingacademy.org

National College for Leadership of Schools and Children's Services
www.nationalcollege.org.uk

Parental Involvement
www.standards.dfes.gov.uk/parentalinvolvement

Parenting UK
www.parentinguk.org

Respect
www.asb.homeoffice.gov.uk

Sure Start Children's Centres
www.dcsf.gov.uk/everychildmatters/earlyyears/surestart/
whatsurestartdoes

Think Family Toolkit
www.dcsf.gov.uk/everychildmatters/strategy/parents/ID91askclient/
thinkfamily/tf

Training and Development Agency for Schools
www.tda.gov.uk

Victoria Climbié Inquiry
www.victoria-climbie-inquiry.org.uk

Further reading

Barrett, H. (2006) *Attachment and the Perils of Parenting*. Sudbury: NFPI (Family and Parenting Institute) Publications.

Bornstein, M.H. (ed.) (1991) *Cultural Approaches to Parenting*. Hillsdale, NJ: Lawrence Erlbaum.

Braun, D. and Schonveld, A. (1993) *Approaching Parenthood: A Resource for Parent Education*. London: Health Education Authority.

Cabinet Office Social Exclusion Task Force (2007) *Reaching Out: Think Family: Analysis and Themes from the Families at Risk Review*. London: Cabinet Office.

Department for Children, Schools and Families (DCSF) (2009) *Think Family Toolkit: Improving Support for Families at Risk*, DCSF 00685-2009. London: DCSF.

Department for Education and Skills (2007) *Every Parent Matters*. London: DfES.

Feeney, J.A., Hohaus, L., Noller, P. and Alexander, R.P. (2001) *Becoming Parents: Exploring the Bonds Between Mothers, Fathers, and Their Infants*. Cambridge: Cambridge University Press.

Gauthier, A.H. (1998) *The State and the Family: A Comparative Analysis of Family Policies in Industrialized Countries*. Oxford: Clarendon Paperbacks.

Hellinckx, W., Colton, M. and Williams, M. (eds) (1997) *International Perspectives on Family Support*. Aldershot: Arena.

May, P. (2005) *Approaching Fatherhood: A Guide for Adoptive Dads and Others*. London: British Association for Adoption and Fostering.

Morgan, P.M. (1995) *Farewell to the Family? Public Policy and Family Breakdown in Britain and the USA*. London: Health and Welfare Unit, Institute of Economic Affairs.

Richardson, J. and Joughlin, C. (2002) *Parent-Training Programmes for the Management of Young Children with Conduct Disorders*. London: Gaskell.

Rosenzweig, J.M. and Brenman, E.M. (eds) (2008) *Work, Life and the Mental Health System of Care: A Guide for Professionals Supporting Families of Children with Emotional or Behavioural Disorders*. Baltimore, MD: Paul H. Brookes.

Saffron, L. (1994) *Challenging Conceptions: Pregnancy and Parenting Beyond the Traditional Family*. London: Cassell.

Sharry, J. (1999) *Bringing Up Responsible Children*. Dublin: Veritas.

Sweet, C. (2001) *Birth Begins at Forty: Challenges the Myths about Late Motherhood*. London: Hodder & Stoughton.

Wachs, T.D. (1992) *The Nature of Nurture*. Newbury Park, CA: Sage.

Winnicott, D.W. (2006) *The Family and Individual Development*. London: Routledge.

Woodward, J. (1998) *The Lone Twin: A Study in Bereavement and Loss*. London: Free Association Books.

References

Barrett, H. (2003) *Parenting Programmes for Families At Risk: A Source Book*. London: National Family and Parenting Institute.

Baumrind, D. (1966) Effects of authoritative parental control on child behaviour. *Child Development* 37 (4): 887–907.

Baumrind, D. (1967) Child care practices anteceding three patterns of preschool behaviour. *Genetic Psychology Monographs* 75 (1): 43–88.

Bayley, R. and Featherstone, S. (2005) *Boys and Girls Come Out to Play: Not Better or Worse, Just Different*. Husbands Bosworth, Leics.: Featherstone Education.

Bettelheim, B. (1987) *A Good Enough Parent: The Guide to Bringing Up Your Child*. London: Central Council for Education and Training in Social Work.

Bowlby, J. (1997) *Attachment*. London: Pimlico.

Burniat, W., Cole, T.J. and Lissau, I. (eds) (2006) *Child and Adolescent Obesity: Causes, Consequences, Prevention and Management*. Cambridge: Cambridge University Press.

Cabinet Office (2008) *Strengthening Leadership in the Public Sector: A Report by the Performance and Innovation Unit (PIU)*. Available at www.cabinetoffice.gov.uk/media/cabinetoffice/strategy/assets/piu leadership.pdf (accessed 22 February 2010).

Coalition on Men and Boys (2009) *Man Made: Men, Masculinities and Equality in Public Policy*. Available at www.comab.org.uk (accessed 22 February 2010).

Crompton, R. (ed.) (1999) *Restructuring Gender Relations and Employment: The Decline of the Male Breadwinner*. Oxford: Oxford University Press.

Department for Children, Schools and Families (DCSF) (2007) *The Children's Plan*. Available at www.dcsf.gov.uk/childrensplan (accessed 22 February 2010).

Department for Children, Schools and Families (DCSF) (2009a) *Common Assessment Framework (CAF)*. Available at www.dcsf.gov.uk/everychildmatters/strategy/deliveringservices1/caf/cafframework (accessed 22 February 2010).

Department for Children, Schools and Families (DCSF) (2009b) *Contact-Point*. Available at www.dcsf.gov.uk/everychildmatters/strategy/

deliveringservices1/contactpoint/contactpoint (accessed 22 February 2010).

Department for Children, Schools and Families (DCSF) (2009c) *Parenting Outcomes Framework for London*. Available at www.younglondon matters.org/uploads/documents/parentingoutcomesframeworkfor london.pdf (accessed 22 February 2010).

Department for Children, Schools and Families (DCSF) (2009d) *Think Family Toolkit: Improving Support for Families at Risk*, DCSF 00685-2009. London: DCSF.

Department for Children, Schools and Families (DCSF) (2010a) *A Timeline of Events Marking Parenting Policy*. Available at www.familyandparenting.org/parentingPolicyTenYears (accessed 28 February 2010).

Department for Children, Schools and Families (DCSF) (2010b) *Family Learning: Helping You to Help Your Child Learn*. Available at www.familylearning.org.uk (accessed 22 February 2010).

Department for Children, Schools and Families (DCSF) (2010c) *Family Pathfinders and Young Carers*. Available at www.dcsf.gov.uk/every childmatters/strategy/parents/pathfinders/familypathfinders (accessed 22 February 2010).

Department for Children, Schools and Families (DCSF) (2010d) *Managers and Leaders*. Available at www.everychildmatters/strategy/managers andleaders (accessed 28 February 2010).

Department for Children, Schools and Families (DCSF) (2010e) *Parental Involvement*. Available at www.standards.dfes.gov.uk/parental involvement (accessed 22 February 2010).

Department for Children, Schools and Families (DCSF) (2010f) *Sure Start Children's Centres*. Available at www.dcsf.gov.uk/everychild matters/earlyyears/surestart/whatsurestartdoes (accessed 22 February 2010).

Department for Education and Skills (DfES) (2003) *Every Child Matters*. Available at www.dcsf.gov.uk/everychildmatters (accessed 22 February 2010).

Department for Education and Skills (DfES) (2007) *Every Parent Matters*. Available at www.dcsf.gov.uk/everychildmatters/resources-and-practice/IG00219 (accessed 22 February 2010).

Dwivedi, K.N. (1997) *Enhancing Parenting Skills: A Guide for Professionals Working with Parents*. Chichester: Wiley.

Fatherhood Institute (2009) *Dad Test and Logbook*. Available at www.fatherhoodinstitute.org/index.php?id=0&cID=1012 (accessed 22 February 2010).

Friedman, M. (2005) *Trying Hard is Not Good Enough*. New Bern, NC: Trafford.

Ghate, D. and Hazel, N. (2002) *Parenting in Poor Environments: Stress, Support and Coping*. London: Jessica Kingsley Publishers.

Gladwell, M. (2000) *The Tipping Point: How Little Things Can Make a Big Difference*. Boston, MA: Little, Brown.

Golding, K. (2000) Parent management training as an intervention to promote adequate parenting. *Clinical Child Psychology and Psychiatry* 5: 357–371.

Goldman, R. (2005) *Fathers' Involvement in Their Children's Education: A Review of Research and Practice*. London: National Family and Parenting Institute.

Gottman, J. (1997) *Raising an Emotionally Intelligent Child*. Seattle, WA: Gottman Institute.

Grimshaw, R. and McGuire, C. (1998) *Evaluating Parenting Programmes: A Study of Stakeholders' Views*. London: National Children's Bureau Enterprises.

Haimowitz, A.G. (2009) *Heredity Versus Environment: Twin, Adoption, and Family Studies*. Available at www.personalityresearch.org/papers/ haimowitz.html (accessed 22 February 2010).

Home Office (2005) *Tackling Anti-social Behaviour and its Causes: The Respect Agenda*. Available at www.asb.homeoffice.gov.uk (accessed 22 February 2010).

Hosseini, K. (2003) *The Kite Runner*. New York: Riverhead Books.

James, A. and Prout, A. (eds) (1997) *Constructing and Reconstructing Childhood*. London: Falmer Press.

Johnson, M.H. (ed.) (1993) *Brain Development and Cognition: A Reader*. Oxford: Blackwell.

Kazdin, A.E. (1997) Parent management training: evidence, outcomes and issues. *Journal of American Academy of Child and Adolescent Psychiatry* 36: 1349–1356.

Kelly, G.A. (1963) *A Theory of Personality: The Psychology of Personal Constructs*. New York: Norton.

Kitzinger, S. (1990) *The Crying Baby*. London: Penguin.

Laming, Lord (2003) *The Victoria Climbié Inquiry*. Available at www.victoria-climbie-inquiry.org.uk (accessed 22 February 2010).

Layard, P.R.G. and Dunn, J. (2009) *A Good Childhood: Searching for Values in a Competitive Age*. London: Penguin.

Lee, H. (2004 [1960]) *To Kill a Mockingbird*. New York: Vintage.

Lindsay, G., Band, S., Cullen, M-A. and Cullen, S. (2008) *Parenting Early Intervention Pathfinder Evaluation*. Available at www.dcsf.gov.uk/

research/data/uploadfiles/DCSF-RW036.pdf (accessed 22 February 2010).

Martin, K., Lord, P., White, R. and Atkinson, M. (2007) *Narrowing the Gap in Outcomes: Leadership*. Slough: NFER. Available at www.c4eo. org.uk/narrowingthegap/files/ntg_leadership_report.pdf (accessed 22 February 2010).

Miller, S. and Sambell, K. (2003) What do parents feel they need? Implications of parents' perspectives for the facilitation of parenting programmes. *Children and Society* 17: 32–44.

National Academy for Parenting Practitioners (NAPP) (2009) *National Academy for Parenting Practitioners*. Available at www.parenting academy. org (accessed 22 February 2010).

National Academy for Parenting Practitioners (NAPP) (2010) *NAPP Commissioning Toolkit*. Available at www.parentingacademy/org/ knowledge/toolkit/commissioners.aspx (accessed 28 February 2010).

Parenting UK (2010) *National Occupational Standards for Work with Parents*. Available at www.parentinguk.org/2/standards (accessed 22 February 2010).

Poskitt, E. and Edmunds, L. (2008) *Management of Childhood Obesity*. Cambridge: Cambridge University Press.

Pugh, G., De'Ath, E. and Smith, C. (1994) *Confident Parents, Confident Children*. London: National Children's Bureau.

Smith, C. (1996) *Developing Parenting Programmes*. London: National Children's Bureau.

Timimi, S. (2005) *Naughty Boys: Antisocial Behaviour, ADHD and the Role of Culture*. Basingstoke: Palgrave Macmillan.

Tovey, H. (2007) *Playing Outdoors, Spaces and Places, Risks and Challenges*. Maidenhead: Open University Press.

Training and Development Agency for Schools (TDA) (2009) *The Parent Support Adviser (PSA) Project*. Available at www.tda.gov.uk/remodelling/ extendedschools/whatarees/parentingsupport/psa_project.aspx (accessed 22 February 2010).

Wolfendale, S. (2002) *Parent Partnership Services for Special Educational Needs: Celebrations and Challenges*. London: David Fulton.

Index

Locators shown in *italics* refer to case studies.

Related books from Open University Press

Purchase from www.openup.co.uk or order through your local bookseller

DEVELOPING MULTIPROFESSIONAL TEAMWORK FOR INTEGRATED CHILDREN'S SERVICES SECOND EDITION

Angela Anning, David Cottrell, Nick Frost, Jo Green and Mark Robinson

This book is an important practical resource for all professionals engaged with planning, implementing and evaluating multi-professional teamwork and practice in children's services.

The first book to combine theoretical perspectives, research evidence from the 'real world' of children's services, and reflections on policy and practice in inter-agency services in England, this fully updated new edition retains its popular approach, while reflecting the numerous changes to policy, practice, and research. The book:

- Exemplifies what multi-professional work looks like in practice
- Examines real dilemmas faced by professionals trying to make it work, and shows how these dilemmas can be resolved
- Considers lessons to be learnt, implications for practice and recommendations for making multi-professional practice effective

Featuring useful guidance, theoretical frameworks and evidence-based insights into practice, this book is a key resource for students on courses studying early childhood and families, as well as social workers, teachers, support workers in children's centres, family support workers, health workers, and managers of a range of children and youth services.

Contents
Acknowledgements – Part 1: Researching and understanding multi-professional teams: working with children – Working in a multi-professional world – Researching multi-professional teams – Organizing and managing multi-professional teams – Part 2: Working and learning in a multi-professional team – Multi-professional perspectives on childhood – Changing roles and responsibilities in multi-professional teams – Sharing knowledge in the multi-professional workplace – Part 3: Planning, implementing and supporting multi-professional teams working with children – Making it work 1 – addressing key dilemmas – Making it work 2 – strategies for decision-making and service delivery – Taking multi-professional practice forward – Appendix: Multi-agency team checklist – Bibliography – Index

June 2010   168pp
978–0–335–23811–8 (Paperback)

PARENTS MATTER
SUPPORTING THE BIRTH TO THREE MATTERS FRAMEWORK

Lesley Abbott and Ann Langston

This book explores the important role of parents and the extended family in the lives of babies and young children. It complements and extends the DfES Birth to Three Matters framework, which supports practitioners in working with children aged birth to three, and builds on the information provided in the companion book *Birth to Three Matters: Supporting the Framework of Effective Practice* (Open University Press, 2004).

Written by academics, practitioners and policy makers interested or involved in the development of the Birth to Three Matters framework, this book argues that parent engagement is essential for developing partnerships within communities in order to give children the best start in life, and shows how this can be achieved. The book:

- Discusses ways in which services may be developed to involve parents more fully in the care and education of babies and young children
- Looks at the powerful role of parents and grandparents in the lives of children
- Considers how skilled practitioners can manage relationships to provide support for both parents and children at difficult times
- Explores the ways in which parents can be helped to fulfil their own needs at the same time as meeting their children's needs
- Includes discussion of families whose children have special needs or disabilities

Parents Matter is essential reading for early years professionals and students on courses in Early Education, as well as policy makers, professional development trainers, local authority trainers, social workers and health visitors who work with very young children.

Contents
List of contributors – Preface – Acknowledgements – Why parents matter – Becoming a family – Grandparents matter – Everyday activities at home: meeting our developmental needs with our young children – 'Don't you tell me what to do' – Parents and child protection matter – Evaluating 'better beginnings' – Health matters to families – 'Arty farty nonsense?' Working with parents in the art gallery – Special lives: Working with parents of children with special educational needs and disabilities – 'Observe more... do less": The approaches of Magda Gerber to parent education – Young parents matter – Children and parents matter: Research insights from integrated child and family services in Australia – Future matters – Index

2006   200pp
978–0–335–21980–3 (Paperback)

MULTIPROFESSIONAL COMMUNICATION
MAKING SYSTEMS WORK FOR CHILDREN

Georgina Glenny and Caroline Roaf

2009 NASEN Award Winner!

- What are the features of successful multiprofessional work?
- How can schools, local authorities and individual fieldworkers work effectively to achieve the best possible outcomes for the children and families with whom they are working?
- How can the Every Child Matters policy agenda be implemented successfully?

This book examines a series of case studies of multiprofessional work, in order to understand what works and why. In the successful case studies, the fieldworkers were able to reflect on the organisational contexts in which they were operating. This was achieved through a carefully managed series of feedback loops, which ensured that good quality information was shared at all levels. With an effective communication system in place they could resolve difficulties and evolve new ways of working together to improve their joint practice.

Multiprofessional Communication is important reading for students on courses with a focus on multiprofessional working, as well as practitioners and policy makers in Education, Health and Social Care.

Contents
List of figures and tables – Acknowledgements – Introduction – The challenge of multiprofessional working – The research base: exploring multiprofessional communication systems in action – Evolving a communication system – Customizing provision to meet local needs – Achieving a positive problem solving culture – The importance of relationships in the field – Conclusions: the dynamics of complexity – References – Index.

2008   152pp
978–0–335–22856–0 (Paperback)   978–0–335–22855–3 (Hardback)